For ResEdit 2.1 ResEdit™ Reference

Addison-Wesley Publishing Company, Inc.

Reading, Massachusetts   Menlo Park, California   New York
Don Mills, Ontario   Wokingham, England   Amsterdam   Bonn
Sidney   Singapore   Tokyo   Madrid   San Juan   Paris
Seoul   Milan   Mexico City   Taipei

APPLE COMPUTER, INC.

© 1991, Apple Computer, Inc.
All rights reserved.

No part of this publication may be reproduced, stored in a retrieval system, or transmitted, in any form or by any means, mechanical, electronic, photocopying, recording, or otherwise, without prior written permission of Apple Computer, Inc. Printed in the United States of America.

Apple Computer, Inc.
20525 Mariani Avenue
Cupertino, CA 95014-6299
408-996-1010

APDA, Apple, the Apple logo, LaserWriter, and Macintosh are registered trademarks of Apple Computer, Inc.

ResEdit is a trademark of Apple Computer, Inc.

ITC Garamond and ITC Zapf Dingbats are registered trademarks of International Typeface Corporation.

Microsoft is a registered trademark of Microsoft Corporation.

PostScript is a registered trademark and Illustrator is a trademark of Adobe Systems Incorporated.

Simultaneously published in the United States and Canada.

ISBN 0-201-57767-4 (without disk)
ISBN 0-201-57768-2 (with disk)

45678910-AL-9594939291,
FOURTH PRINTING SEPTEMBER 1991

LIMITED WARRANTY ON MEDIA AND REPLACEMENT

ALL IMPLIED WARRANTIES ON THIS MANUAL, INCLUDING IMPLIED WARRANTIES OF MERCHANTABILITY AND FITNESS FOR A PARTICULAR PURPOSE, ARE LIMITED IN DURATION TO NINETY (90) DAYS FROM THE DATE OF THE ORIGINAL RETAIL PURCHASE OF THIS PRODUCT.

Even though Apple has reviewed this manual, **APPLE MAKES NO WARRANTY OR REPRESENTATION, EITHER EXPRESS OR IMPLIED, WITH RESPECT TO THIS MANUAL, ITS QUALITY, ACCURACY, MERCHANTABILITY, OR FITNESS FOR A PARTICULAR PURPOSE. AS A RESULT, THIS MANUAL IS SOLD "AS IS," AND YOU, THE PURCHASER, ARE ASSUMING THE ENTIRE RISK AS TO ITS QUALITY AND ACCURACY.**

IN NO EVENT WILL APPLE BE LIABLE FOR DIRECT, INDIRECT, SPECIAL, INCIDENTAL, OR CONSEQUENTIAL DAMAGES RESULTING FROM ANY DEFECT OR INACCURACY IN THIS MANUAL, even if advised of the possibility of such damages.

THE WARRANTY AND REMEDIES SET FORTH ABOVE ARE EXCLUSIVE AND IN LIEU OF ALL OTHERS, ORAL OR WRITTEN, EXPRESS OR IMPLIED. No Apple dealer, agent, or employee is authorized to make any modification, extension, or addition to this warranty.

Some states do not allow the exclusion or limitation of implied warranties or liability for incidental or consequential damages, so the above limitation or exclusion may not apply to you. This warranty gives you specific legal rights, and you may also have other rights which vary from state to state.

Contents

Figures and tables / viii

Preface / xi
Prerequisites / xii
What this manual contains / xii
How to use this manual / xii
Conventions used in this book / xiii
Graphics / xiii
Where to get information / xiii
    About APDA / xiv
    About Developer Programs / xiv

1 ResEdit Overview / 1
Resources / 2
    New and changed resource editors in ResEdit 2.1 / 3
Editing resources in ResEdit / 4
Uses / 4
Extensibility / 5
The resource development cycle / 5

2 Getting Started / 7
Invoking ResEdit / 8
Working with files / 9
    Resource checking / 9
    Opening a file / 10
Menus in ResEdit / 12
    The File menu / 13
        File information / 16
    The Edit menu / 17
    The Resource menu / 18
    The Window menu / 22

The View menu / 23
Starting an editor / 25
Resource ID numbers / 25

3 The Bit Editors / 27

Overview of the bit editors / 28
   Tools / 29
   Menus / 30
      The Transform menu / 30
      The Color menu / 31
Editing cursors / 33
Editing icons / 35
   Editing 'cicn' resources / 35
      The cicn menu / 36
      Creating new color icons / 36
   Finder icons / 36
      The Icon menu / 38
   'ICON' resources / 39
   'ICN#' resources / 39
List resources / 41
   'SICN' resources / 41
Editing Patterns / 42
   Relative patterns / 43
   Custom patterns / 43
   'PAT' resources / 44
   'PAT#' resources / 44
   'ppat' resources / 45
     'ppat' relative patterns / 45
   'ppt#' resources / 46
      Desktop pattern lists / 46
     'ppt#' relative patterns / 47
'FONT' resources / 47
   Editing 'FONT' resources / 48

4 Other Resource Editors / 51

Using the hexadecimal editor / 52
'WIND', 'ALRT', and 'DLOG' resources / 53
'DITL' resources / 59

'BNDL' resources / 64
'clut' and 'pltt' resources / 68
'INTL', 'itl0', and 'itl1' resources / 70
'KCHR' resources / 71
   The main 'KCHR' editor / 72
      The character chart / 72
      The table chart / 73
      The virtual keycode chart / 73
      The keyboard region / 74
      The information region / 74
   Editing dead keys / 75
   The dead-key editor / 75
      The character chart / 75
      The nomatch character / 76
      The completion and substitution character pair list / 76
      The Trash / 76
      The information region / 76
   The menus / 77
      The KCHR menu / 77
      The Font menu / 79
      The Size menu / 79
'MENU' resources / 79
'TEXT' and 'styl' resources / 84
'vers' resources / 85

5 ResEdit Templates / 87

Template characteristics / 88
Editing / 89
   'PICT' editing / 89
Creating new templates / 90
   Template example / 91

6 ResEdit Tips / 95

Hints and kinks / 96
   The 'LAYO' resource / 99
   'KCHR' questions and answers / 105

7 The Programmatic Interface / 107

Pickers and editors / 108
Code-containing resources in the ResEdit release / 108
    Samples / 108
        Sample editor / 109
        Sample picker / 109
        Sample LDEF / 109
    Building the examples / 110
Using ResEd / 110
Writing a ResEdit extension / 111
    ResEdit Menus / 111
    Pickers / 112
    ResEdit 2.0 changes / 112
    ResEd changes for the 2.0 release / 113
    ResEdit 2.1 changes / 113
    Required routines / 115
The ResEd interface / 117
    Data structures / 118
        The parent record / 119
        The picker record / 120
    Other routines / 120
        Window utilities / 121
        Extended resource manager / 124
        Routines used by pickers / 126
        Routines used by editors / 128
        Routines used to start pickers and editors / 129
        Routines used to feed events and menus to the appropriate picker or editor / 130
        Miscellaneous utilities / 130
        Pop-up menus / 137
        Internal routines / 138

A The 'KCHR' Resource / 143

Basic theory of keyboard operation / 144
    Generating the virtual keycode / 144
        Exceptions to the rule / 144
    Generating the character code / 144
    Dead keys / 145
The structure of a 'KCHR' resource / 146

B The 'BNDL' Resource / 149

The structure of a 'BNDL' resource / 150

Definitions of the 'BNDL' and 'FREF' resources / 153

C Resource Types Defined for / 155

D The Macintosh Character Set / 161

Index / 163

Figures and tables

2 Getting Started / 7

Figure 2-1   ResEdit's startup display / 8
Figure 2-2   ResEdit File Open dialog box / 9
Figure 2-3   Add Resource Fork alert box / 10
Figure 2-4   A ResEdit 2.1 file window / 11
Figure 2-5   File menu / 13
Figure 2-6   Open Special dialog box / 15
Figure 2-7   A File Info window / 15
Figure 2-8   A Folder Info window / 16
Figure 2-9   Preferences dialog box / 17
Figure 2-10   Edit menu / 18
Figure 2-11   File window Resource menu with 'BNDL' type selected / 18
Figure 2-12   The Resource menu with a picker open / 19
Figure 2-13   There is no template for 'CODE' resources / 20
Figure 2-14   An 'ICN#' Get Info window / 21
Figure 2-15   A resource type window (with custom picker) / 21
Figure 2-16   The Window menu / 23
Figure 2-17   The View menu and a ResEdit 2.1 file window / 23
Figure 2-18   The View menu and a resource type window / 24
Figure 2-19   Showing type attributes / 24

3 The Bit Editors / 27

Figure 3-1   Bit editor window layout / 28
Figure 3-2   The Transform menu / 30
Figure 3-3   The Color menu / 31
Figure 3-4   'CURS' resource editor / 33
Figure 3-5   Color cursor editing mask examples / 34
Figure 3-6   Color icon editor / 35
Figure 3-7   Finder icon family editor / 37
Figure 3-8   Icon menu / 38
Figure 3-9   'ICON' resource editor / 39
Figure 3-10   'ICN#' resource editor / 40
Figure 3-11   'SICN' resource editor / 41

Figure 3-12 Pattern Size dialog box / 42
Figure 3-13 'PAT' resource editor / 44
Figure 3-14 'PAT#' resource editor / 44
Figure 3-15 'ppat' resource editor / 45
Figure 3-16 'ppt#' resource editor / 46
Figure 3-17 'FONT' resource editor / 49

4 Other Resource Editors / 51

Figure 4-1 'WIND' resource editor / 54
Figure 4-2 MiniScreen menu / 54
Figure 4-3 'ALRT' resource editor / 55
Figure 4-4 'DLOG' resource editor / 55
Figure 4-5 WIND menu / 56
Figure 4-6 Setting 'WIND' characteristics / 57
Figure 4-7 ALRT menu / 57
Figure 4-8 'ALRT' Stage Info dialog box / 58
Figure 4-9 DLOG menu / 58
Figure 4-10 setting 'DLOG' characteristics / 59
Figure 4-11 'DITL' resource editor / 60
Figure 4-12 'DITL' item editor / 61
Figure 4-13 DITL menu / 61
Figure 4-14 DITL menu View As dialog box / 63
Figure 4-15 Alignment menu / 63
Figure 4-16 Special parameter strings / 64
Figure 4-17 'BNDL' resource editor, simple view / 65
Figure 4-18 The Icon chooser / 66
Figure 4-19 'BNDL' resource editor, extended view / 67
Figure 4-20 'clut' resource editor / 68
Figure 4-21 clut menu / 69
Figure 4-22 Editing an 'itl0' resource / 70
Figure 4-23 Editing an 'itl1' resource / 71
Figure 4-24 Editing a 'KCHR' resource / 72
Figure 4-25 Editing a dead key / 75
Figure 4-26 The KCHR menu / 77
Figure 4-27 Dead Key Edit Dialog Box / 78
Figure 4-28 'MENU' resource editor / 80
Figure 4-29 'MENU' line item edit / 81

Figure 4-30 'MENU' Mark pop-up menu / 81
Figure 4-31 'MENU' Icon Chooser dialog box / 82
Figure 4-32 Editing a 'cmnu' resource / 83
Figure 4-33 'MENU' ID dialog box / 84
Figure 4-34 'TEXT' and 'styl' editor / 84
Figure 4-35 Editing a 'vers' resource / 85

5 ResEdit Templates / 87

Figure 5-1 The template editor for 'PICT' / 90
Figure 5-2 'TMPL' definition for type 'STR#' / 91
Figure 5-3 'STR#' template in use / 91

6 ResEdit Tips / 95

Figure 6-1 'RMAP' resource / 99
Figure 6-2 'LAYO' template, view 1 / 100
Figure 6-3 'LAYO' template, view 2 / 101
Figure 6-4 'LAYO' template, view 3 / 102
Figure 6-5 'LAYO' template, view 4 / 103
Figure 6-6 'LAYO' template, view 5 / 104

A The 'KCHR' Resource / 143

Figure A-1 Modifier flag high byte / 147

B The 'BNDL' Resource / 149

Figure B-1 Six resources and their relationships / 151

C Resource Types Defined for Rez and ResEdit / 155

Table C-1 Resource types defined for Rez and ResEdit / 156

D The Macintosh Character Set / 161

Figure D-1 Macintosh character set / 162

Preface

ResEdit™, an extensible stand-alone resource editor for the Macintosh® computer, is a powerful tool you can use to speed your software development process and to create icons, menus, and other resources for Macintosh programs and files. This manual is a complete reference to ResEdit that includes introductions to the various resource type editors included in the program and a discussion of the framework that is provided so that you can extend the capabilities of the program by adding your own resource pickers and editors.

Prerequisites

To run ResEdit 2.1, the system you use must have at least 128 kilobytes of ROM and at least 1 megabyte of RAM memory. That is, ResEdit 2.1 doesn't run on the Macintosh Plus or earlier machines.

ResEdit 2.1 works with system software version 6.0 and later. ResEdit is compatible with (but does not require) 32-bit QuickDraw™.

What this manual contains

Chapter 1 introduces the concepts behind ResEdit, starting with an overview of Macintosh resources. Chapter 2 tells you about the user interface. Chapter 3 discusses the editors in ResEdit that handle various kinds of bitmap resources (cursors, icons, and so on), and Chapter 4 discusses the other built-in editors. Chapter 5 describes template editing and tells you how to build your own templates. Chapter 6 contains "hints and kinks" — useful information that will help you make efficient use of ResEdit. Chapter 7 describes the programmatic interface to ResEdit and tells you what you need to know to write your own picker or editor. Appendix A describes the inner workings of the 'KCHR' editor, Appendix B describes the inner workings of the 'BNDL' resource, Appendix C lists a number of extant resource types, and Appendix D is a chart of the regular Macintosh character set.

How to use this manual

If you have used previous versions of ResEdit, you will probably want to take a quick look at Chapter 2, which describes the user interface in some detail. The interface has been changed in version 2.0 and, to a lesser extent, in version 2.1.

If you have never used ResEdit, you should probably read Chapters 1 and 2 and look over the rest of the book. Use the program for a while, and then look at the book again. It will probably make a lot more sense after you've actually played with ResEdit.

Conventions used in this book

The following visual cues are used throughout this book to identify different types of information:

- ◆ *Note:* A note like this contains information that is interesting but not essential for an understanding of the main text.

△ **Important**   A note like this contains information that is essential. △

▲ **Warning**   A warning like this indicates potential problems. ▲

This manual uses `courier` type to represent code fragments and the names of procedures.

Graphics

Most of the artwork in this book is taken directly from Macintosh screens. Some illustrations show a condensed version of the screen with a sequence of windows or some particular feature (such as a menu) evident. Others show only an active window or an alert or dialog box.

Where to get information

Apple® technical books published by Addison-Wesley, such as *Inside Macintosh*, are available at commercial bookstores. Books and manuals published by Apple are available through APDA®, the Apple Programmers and Developers Association, at the address listed in the next section. Technical notes and other materials of interest to Macintosh application developers are also available from APDA.

About APDA

APDA provides a wide range of technical products and documentation from Apple Computer, Inc. and other suppliers, for programmers and developers who work on Apple equipment. You can contact them as follows.

APDA
Apple Computer, Inc.
20525 Mariani Avenue, M/S 33-G
Cupertino, CA 95014–6299

Telephone: 1-800-282-APDA or 1-800-282-2732 if you are inside the United States; in Canada, 1-800-637-0029; elsewhere in the world, 01-408-562-3910.
Fax: 408-562-3971   Telex: 171-576   AppleLink: DEV.CHANNELS

About Developer Programs

If you plan to develop hardware or software products for sale through retail channels, you can get valuable support from Apple Developer Programs. Write to them at the following address:

Apple Developer Programs
Apple Computer, Inc.
20525 Mariani Avenue, M/S 75-2C
Cupertino, CA 95014–6299

Chapter 1 ResEdit Overview

This chapter introduces the concept of resources as they are handled on the Macintosh® computer, and introduces ResEdit™, an interactive, graphics-oriented application for manipulating resources in Macintosh files. Some Macintosh files don't contain any resources, but all applications and most of the System Folder files do.

Resources

One of the differences between Macintosh computers and other computers is the way Macintosh machines handle **resources** (typefaces, icons, dialog boxes, and so on). In the Macintosh world, resources are distinct from data (for example, the text in a word-processing file). The Macintosh does not insist that resources reside in a central pool; they may be placed in any file.

In most computers, a file consists of a sequence of bytes, perhaps beginning with a header that contains some information about the structure of the data contained in the file, and possibly ending with some sort of trailer. In any case, the file is one sequence of bytes. In the Macintosh world, by contrast, the file structure is designed to include two sequences of bytes, a **data fork** and a **resource fork**. Any file may contain only a data fork, only a resource fork, or both. Although a plain HyperCard® stack, for example, has only data in it, people commonly add icons and sounds to their stacks, creating resource forks for those stacks in the process.

Resources are classified by type. Each type has its own name, which consists of exactly four characters. Any characters in the Macintosh character set can occur in resource type names, even unprintable ones, but typically they consist of lower and uppercase letters, numerals, punctuation marks, and the space and Option-space characters. In this book, resource type names are surrounded by single straight quotation marks (for example, `'itl0'`). If you see a name that appears to be shorter than four characters (for example, `'snd'`), the empty slots are probably filled with spaces. Some resource types are named and described in Appendix C. There are many different types of resources, and you can create your own resource types with ResEdit if you don't find the type you need.

◆ *Note:* Apple Computer, Inc., reserves all names that don't contain any uppercase letters. Any combination with at least one uppercase letter in it is yours to use, though it is a good idea to avoid using any resource type name that you know someone else has already used.

Another feature of this system is that code is regarded as a resource. It even has its own resource type name (very straightforwardly, `'CODE'`). Any application, then, must have a resource fork, which is where its code resides, along with various other resources, such as menus.

ResEdit lets you copy and paste all resource types and lets you edit many of them. (`'NFNT'` is an exception and is discussed briefly in the section on `'FONT'` editing in Chapter 3.) ResEdit actually includes a number of different resource editors: There is a **general resource editor** for editing any resource in hexadecimal and ASCII formats, and there are individual resource editors for various specific resource types. There is also a **template editor** which lets you edit some kinds of resources in a dialog box format, with fields that you can fill in as appropriate. There are predefined templates for quite a few resources already built into ResEdit, and you can create others. For further information on template editing and on generating your own templates, see Chapter 5.

New and changed resource editors in ResEdit 2.1

ResEdit 2.1 includes new editors for the following resource types:

- `'crsr'` — Color cursors
- `'clut'` and `'pltt'` — Color lookup tables, palettes
- `'ppat'` and `'ppt#'` — Color patterns and pattern lists
- `'styl'`/`'TEXT'` — Styled text
- `'vers'` — Version resource

The editors for the following resource types have been changed:

`'DITL'`	Dialog item list
`'DLOG'`	Dialog box
`'PAT'`	black-and-white pattern
`'PAT#'`	black-and-white pattern list
`'ICON'`	Icons (for instance, HyperCard icons)
`'ICN#'`	Icons (original Finder icons)
`'SICN'`	Small icons
`'CURS'`	black-and-white cursors
`'cicn'`	Color icons

Finder™ icon suite (includes `'ICN#'`, `'icl4'`, `'icl8'`, `'ics#'`, `'ics4'`, and `'ics8'` resources).

Editing resources in ResEdit

ResEdit provides three kinds or categories of resource editors: individual editors, a template editor, and a hexadecimal editor.

Individual resource editors are described in some detail in Chapters 3 and 4. Several of the resources (`'CURS'`, `'FONT'`, `'ICON'`, `'PAT'`, and so on) that are edited with individual editors are graphic or pictorial. To edit any of the pictorial resources except `'PICT'`, you use bit editors, which are discussed in Chapter 3. `'PICT'` resources are special. The individual editor for `'PICT'` resources only displays them; it does not allow you to change them.

Some resources are edited with templates. If you open a resource of this kind, you are presented with a dialog box that contains various labeled fields. You can change the contents of the fields. Information on existing templates and on generating your own templates appears in Chapter 5, and an example of template editing appears in Chapter 6.

To edit resources for which there is no template or individual editor, you must use the hexadecimal editor unless you write your own templates or editors for them.

Uses

ResEdit is especially useful for creating and changing graphic resources, such as dialog boxes and icons. For example, you can use ResEdit to try out different formats and presentations of resources in the process of putting together a quick prototype of a user interface. Anyone can quickly learn to use ResEdit for translating resources into languages other than English without having to recompile programs. You can use ResEdit to modify a program's resources at any stage in the process of program development. ResEdit is also useful for modifying the `'LAYO'` (desktop layout control) resource in a copy of the Finder so that you can reconfigure some aspects of the desktop display. See Chapter 6 for more details about the `'LAYO'` resource.

Extensibility

A key feature of ResEdit is its extensibility. Because it can't anticipate the formats of all the different types of resources that you may use, ResEdit is designed so that you can teach it to recognize and parse new resource types.

There are two ways to extend ResEdit to handle new types:

- You can create templates for your own resource types. ResEdit lets you edit most resource types by filling in the fields of a dialog box; this is the way you edit the Finder's desktop layout control resource, for example. The ordering of the items in these dialog boxes is determined by a template in ResEdit's resource fork, and you can add templates to ResEdit or to the ResEdit Preferences file yourself to edit new resource types. Resource templates are described in Chapter 5, and the desktop layout control resource is discussed in some detail in Chapter 6.

- You can program your own special-purpose **resource picker** or **editor** (or both) and add it to either ResEdit or to the ResEdit Preferences file. (The **resource picker** is the code that displays all the resources of one type in the resource type window. The **editor** is the code that displays and allows you to edit a particular resource. These pieces of code are separate from the main code of ResEdit.) A set of Pascal or C routines, called ResEd, is available for this purpose — see Chapter 7 for information. The advantage of adding your code to the ResEdit Preferences file rather than to ResEdit itself is that doing so facilitates updating to new versions of ResEdit as they become available.

The resource development cycle

ResEdit is often used with Macintosh Programmer's Workshop (MPW®) and other program development systems. Once you have created or modified a resource with ResEdit, you can use the MPW resource decompiler, DeRez, to convert the resource to a textual representation that can be processed by the resource compiler, Rez. You can then add comments to this text file or otherwise modify it with the MPW Shell or another text editor. Rez and DeRez are fully described in the *Macintosh Programmer's Workshop Reference* (*MPW Reference*). It is not necessary to use Rez or DeRez unless you have some specific need or desire to modify or comment the code that DeRez produces; the resources generated by ResEdit are, in general, entirely acceptable.

Chapter 2 **Getting Started**

If you are new to ResEdit, you will want to proceed with some caution, as ResEdit is quite powerful and can easily damage or destroy your files. If you are accustomed to ResEdit versions prior to 2.0, you will notice that the user interface has been extensively changed and now conforms more closely to the guidelines established by Apple Computer, Inc.

Invoking ResEdit

ResEdit is a regular application, so if you are in the Finder or in HyperCard you can start it up just as you would any other application. If you are using MPW, you can start ResEdit by entering either of these commands in the MPW Shell:

```
ResEdit
ResEdit file1 file2 ...
```

The latter command causes ResEdit to open the named files automatically.

When ResEdit first starts up, it displays an animated startup display. Figure 2-1 shows one of the stages of this animation.

■ **Figure 2-1** ResEdit's startup display

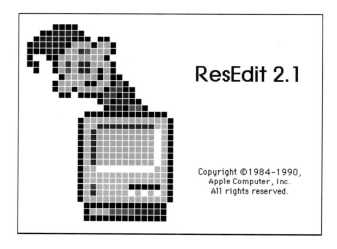

The animation continues until you click the mouse button or press any key. If you click the mouse button or press an unmodified key, ResEdit presents a dialog box, shown in Figure 2-2, that lets you create a new file or open an existing one. If you press a Command-key combination, the startup display is dismissed and ResEdit performs the action you have requested. This is especially useful for Command-key combinations assigned to the Open Special menu, described in this chapter. You can, if you wish, use the Preferences command on the File menu to suppress the dialog box.

■ **Figure 2-2** ResEdit File Open dialog box

You can select a filename by clicking it or by typing one or more characters of the filename.

Working with files

ResEdit provides facilities to let you open and create files and perform two levels of verification on them; it also lets you create, move, and edit resources.

Resource checking

Sometimes a resource file gets corrupted. This is typically the result of a crash occurring while the file is being updated. In the past, ResEdit would occasionally crash when you tried to open a damaged file with it. Versions of ResEdit starting with 2.0 provide resource file checking facilities to help avoid crashes and to minimize loss of data. The checking facility does not detect corrupted individual resources; it bases its tests on the file's resource map.

When you open a file, ResEdit performs a partial resource check on it. This test verifies only that the resource map is located after the end of the resource data area, and that the header, data, and map do not extend beyond the EOF (end-of-file mark) of the resource fork. If the file does not pass these initial tests, a full test is automatically performed. If you choose "Verify files when they are opened" in the Preferences dialog box, ResEdit performs a full test whenever you open a file.

If you want to invoke the full test yourself, choose Verify Resource File from the File menu.

When it performs a full resource check, ResEdit goes through the entire resource map and verifies that the type list, the reference lists, and the name list are consistent, that all resource data areas can be located, and that they do not exceed the available file size. It also checks for duplicate types, and for duplicate ID numbers within each type. ResEdit has several techniques for locating the resource map, the existence and location of which is critical to the process of recovering damaged resource files.

If damage is discovered, the user is offered a repair option. This procedure does not change the damaged file. Instead, ResEdit creates a new file, extracts all the resources it can find in the damaged file, and copies them to the new file. It then renames the old file (with an extension of "(damaged)". ResEdit also presents the user with status information about the resources that were extracted.

There is one exception to the rule that the damaged file is not changed: minor damage occurs whenever a resource file is not properly closed. ResEdit repairs this damage without asking the user's permission. (The actual process involved is quite simple: ResEdit calls the Resource Manager to open the file, calls the `UpdateResFile` routine to rewrite the resource map, and closes the file.) After performing the repair, it presents an alert box to inform the user that it has done so.

Opening a file

To list the resource types in a file, select and open the filename from the list in the File Open dialog box. If you try to open a file that does not have a resource fork, ResEdit displays a dialog box, shown in Figure 2-3, that asks you whether you want to open the file anyway. If you permit it to open the file, ResEdit extends the file by creating a resource fork in it.

■ **Figure 2-3** Add Resource Fork alert box

▲ **Warning** You can edit any file shown in the window, including the System file and ResEdit itself, though there are some restrictions (the Finder and the Desktop file cannot be opened by ResEdit under MultiFinder®, for example). It's dangerous, though, to edit a file that's currently in use. In general, it is much wiser to edit a duplicate instead of the file itself. ▲

When you open a file, a **file window** appears. This window displays a pictorial list of all the resource types in that file (see Figure 2-4), unless you choose "by Type" from the View menu (see Figure 2-18). If you do choose to view the resource list by resource type, you can also choose to show the total size of each resource type.

■ **Figure 2-4** A ResEdit 2.1 file window

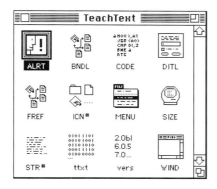

When a file window is the active window, you can create new resource types, copy or delete existing resources, and paste resources from other files into the currently active one. Here, operations are performed on sets of resources. For example, selecting the resource type `'ALRT'` in a file causes all resources of type `'ALRT'` in that file to be selected as a group. Any operation you then perform on that group affects all `'ALRT'` resources in the file. To select more than one resource type, hold down the Command key while clicking the individual items or click an item at the beginning of the range you want to select, hold down the Shift key, and click the item at the end of the range. The Shift key allows you to select the items in a rectangular area. You can then continue to select or deselect individual resource types with the Command key pressed. (These techniques also work for selecting individual resources within an open resource type.)

◆ *Note:* Many applications put more than one resource type at a time into the scrap when Copy is chosen. For example, when an object is copied in MacDraw®, an `'MDPL'` resource and a `'PICT'` resource are put into the scrap. When you paste into the file window in ResEdit, all resources that are present are pasted.

◆ *Note:* Starting with version 2.0, you can no longer use ResEdit to delete files; also, ResEdit does not manipulate or read data forks (this means, for example, that it cannot copy them).

Menus in ResEdit

The structure of menus in ResEdit has been changed with the 2.1 release. Five main menus (File, Edit, Resource, Window, View) are discussed here, and special menus for particular resources are discussed in the sections on editing those resources, in Chapters 3 and 4.

The File menu

Figure 2-5 shows the File menu.

- **Figure 2-5** File menu

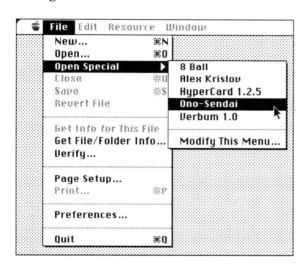

The File menu commands act as follows:

New...	Brings up the New File dialog box.
Open...	Brings up a File Open dialog box similar to the one shown in Figure 2-2, but without a New button.
Open Special	Allows you to open files quickly. The Modify This Menu command, which always appears at the bottom of the submenu, brings up the dialog box shown in Figure 2-6. Use this dialog box to add and remove files and Command-key combinations.
Close	Closes the currently active window. (Using this command has the same effect as clicking the close box.)
Save	Saves the currently active file, if there is one. Dimmed if no changes have been made.
Revert File	Restores the currently active file, if there is one, to the last version you saved. Dimmed if no changes have been made.

Get Info for This File
: When no file is open, this command is dimmed and cannot be used. When a file is open, the words *This File* are replaced by the filename, and this command is enabled. It displays file information and allows you to change it. The file information box is shown in Figure 2-7.

Get File/Folder Info...
: Displays file or folder information and allows you to change it. Figure 2-7 shows a File Info window as it appears under system software version 6.0. Figure 2-8 is a Folder Info window, also for system software version 6.0.

Verify Resource File...
: Allows you to check the resource map of a file you specify.

Page Setup... Brings up the Page Setup dialog box.

Print... Allows you to print from almost any picker or editor. When no files are open, this command is dimmed and cannot be used.

Preferences... Brings up the dialog box shown in Figure 2-9. This lets you specify whether you want ResEdit to show its splash screen (Figure 2-1), whether you want it to start up with a File Open dialog box, whether you want to be warned if you attempt to open the System file or ResEdit itself, and whether you want ResEdit to perform a verify operation on files when you open them. It also allows you to set the sizes of type picker and resource picker windows, or, if you prefer, to let ResEdit automatically fit them to the size of your screen. If you have more than one monitor, it lets you specify whether pickers and editors for color resources should open on the deepest available display or on the main display if they are not the same.

Quit Quits ResEdit and returns to the Finder (or the MPW Shell, HyperCard, or whatever program launched ResEdit).

■ **Figure 2-6** Open Special dialog box

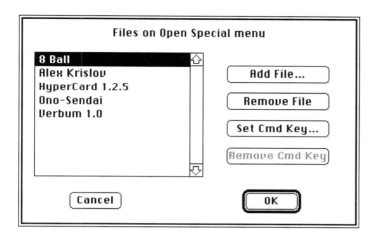

■ **Figure 2-7** A File Info window

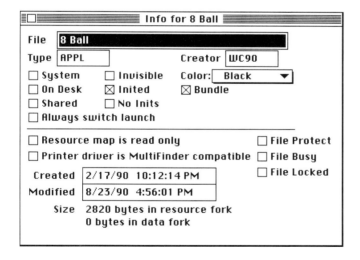

File information

The File Info window contains the following information:

The name of the file; its type and creator; a pop-up menu that lets you set the color in which the file is shown on the screen; two sets of checkboxes (above and below a horizontal line); the creation and modification dates of the file; and the sizes of both forks.

The checkboxes above the horizontal line are known as Finder Flags. Please see *Macintosh Technical Note* 40 and Chapter 9 of *Inside Macintosh,* Volume VI, for more information about Finder Flags in general; Appendix B of this book contains information about how the Bundle bit relates to the 'BNDL' resource.

The checkboxes below the line are as follows: the File Locked bit is the same one that you find in the Finder's Get Info box for the file. The Printer Driver Is MultiFinder Compatible bit means exactly that, and is used only for printer drivers. The File Busy bit is controlled by the operating system. The Resource Map Is Read Only bit can be set in Rez, but not in ResEdit. ResEdit cannot change the File Protected bit.

■ **Figure 2-8** A Folder Info window

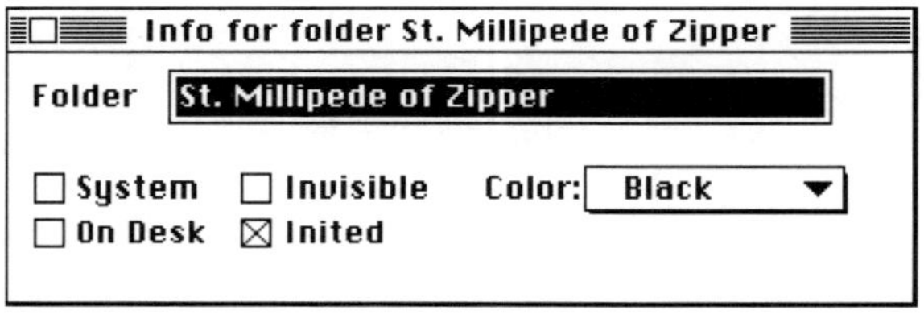

16   ResEdit Reference

■ **Figure 2-9** Preferences dialog box

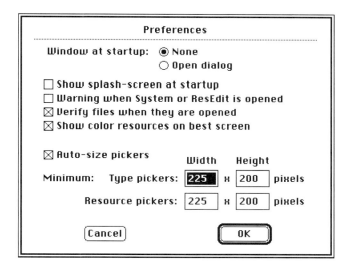

The Edit menu

Figure 2-10 shows the Edit menu. It has only one unusual feature, the Select Changed command on the last line. Choose this command to select only those items that have been changed since the last time you saved your file.

■ **Figure 2-10** Edit menu

The Resource menu

The Resource menu is configured to provide the commands appropriate for the frontmost window. The same items are always present on the menu, but their meanings and wordings may change slightly, depending on the context. The wording of a given menu item always reflects the action that is taken when you choose it. Figure 2-11 shows the Resource menu with a resource type picker open and the 'BNDL' type selected.

■ **Figure 2-11** File window Resource menu with 'BNDL' type selected

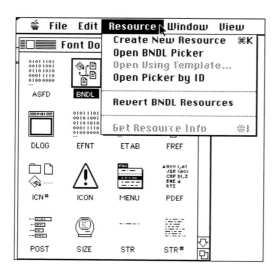

18 ResEdit Reference

The Create New Resource command lets you create any resource type. The Open Picker command invokes a picker for the particular kind of resource that is selected. This is reflected in its name, which includes the name of the selected resource type. The Open Picker by ID command opens the picker window showing the resources ordered by ID number, regardless of what the last View choice was. This is useful if View by Special has problems because of a corrupted resource. At this level, the only other command you can use is the Revert Resources command, which restores the resources to their state in the last saved version of the file. If you have made changes in individual resources of the selected type since you last saved the file, you can undo those changes at this point.

Figure 2-12 shows the Resource menu again, this time with a resource picker open. Note that it is now possible to open a resource with a resource editor or template (if one is available) or with the hexadecimal editor.

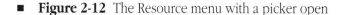
■ **Figure 2-12** The Resource menu with a picker open

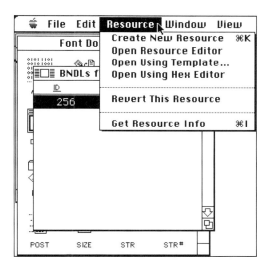

Figure 2-13 shows the result of attempting to use the Open Using Template command on a `CODE` resource. There is, in fact, no template for resources of this type. It is generally not useful to open a resource of one type with a template for a resource of a different type.

■ **Figure 2-13** There is no template for `'CODE'` resources

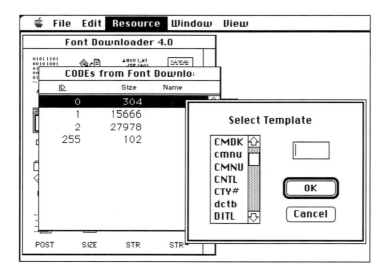

It is also possible to get information on the selected resource. Figure 2-14 shows the Get Info window for a resource of type `'ICN#'`. This dialog box lets you change the name and ID number of the resource, and select or deselect some of its attributes.

- **System Heap:** If this attribute is set, the resource is placed in the system heap unless it is too large to fit. In that case, the resource is placed in the application heap, as if the box were not checked. This attribute should not be set for an application's resources.
- **Purgeable:** If this attribute is set, the resource can be purged from memory if more room is needed. It is typically a good idea to set this attribute.
- **Locked:** If this attribute is set, the resource is locked in place in the heap and cannot be moved. This attribute overrides the Purgeable attribute.
- **Protected:** If this attribute is set, the Resource Manager cannot change the name or ID number of the resource, modify its contents, or remove the resource from the file that contains it. The toolbox routine that sets these attributes can be called, however, to unset this one.
- **Preload:** Setting this attribute causes the Resource Manager to load the resource into memory immediately after opening the resource file.

■ **Figure 2-14** An 'ICN#' Get Info window

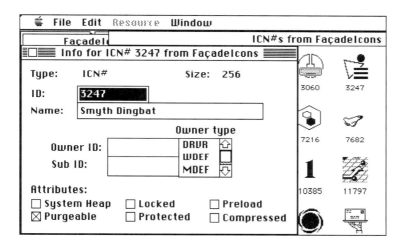

Opening a resource type produces a window that lists each resource of that type in the file. The list is generated by a resource picker and will take different forms, depending on the particular resource picker that is displaying it. The general resource picker displays the resources by type, name, ID number, or order in the file; pickers for specific resource types generate displays that are appropriate for their type. Figure 2-15 shows a picker for the 'ICN#' resource type.

You can also write your own pickers. For more information, see Chapter 7.

■ **Figure 2-15** A resource type window (with custom picker)

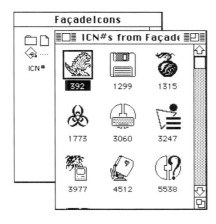

Chapter 2 Getting Started   21

When a resource type window is the active window, the Edit menu commands have the following effects:

Undo — Not usable.

Cut — Removes the resources that are selected, placing them in the ResEdit scrap. If only one resource is selected, it is placed on the Clipboard.

Copy — Copies all the resources that are selected into the ResEdit scrap. If only one resource is selected, it is copied to the Clipboard.

Paste — Copies the resources from the ResEdit scrap (or from the Clipboard) into the resource type window.

◆ *Note:* Only resources of the currently open type are copied into the resource type window.

Clear — Removes the resources that are selected without placing them in the ResEdit scrap.

Duplicate — Creates a duplicate of the selected resources and assigns a unique resource ID number to each new resource.

When you choose Open Using Template from the Resource menu, a list of templates is displayed, and you can pick the one you want to use.

The Window menu

The Window menu, shown in Figure 2-16, gives you an overview of what windows are currently open and indicates the currently active window with a checkmark. It also lets you select a new current window. Note that the Window menu is sorted by file rather than by how close to the front a particular window is.

■ **Figure 2-16** The Window menu

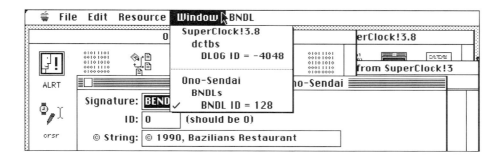

The View menu

The View menu is configured to match the frontmost window. When a file window is currently active, the View menu lets you show the resource types in a file by icon or type name, and if you show them by type, it lets you show the size of each type (that is, the sum of the sizes of all resources within the type). See Figure 2-17.

■ **Figure 2-17** The View menu and a ResEdit 2.1 file window

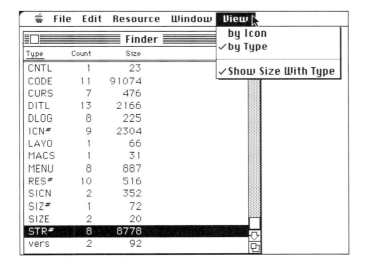

When a resource type window is the currently active window, the View menu lets you choose among several viewing styles (see Figure 2-18) and lets you show some attributes for each resource when you view by ID, Name, Size, or Order in File (see Figure 2-19). Attributes can be displayed but cannot be edited when you use the Show Attributes command.

For some resources, the "by Special" line is changed to a type-specific alternate (for example, "by cicn", as shown in Figure 2-18). Attributes cannot be displayed in the special views.

When an individual resource is open, the View menu is not shown.

- **Figure 2-18** The View menu and a resource type window

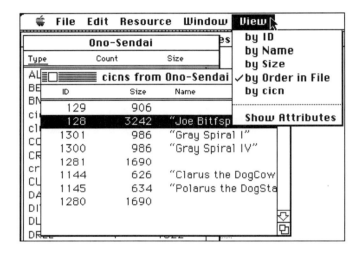

- **Figure 2-19** Showing type attributes

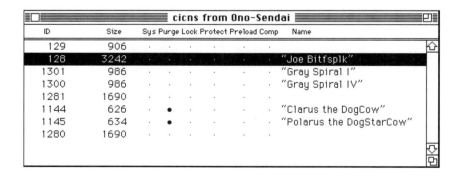

Starting an editor

To open an editor for a particular resource in a file, first open the picker for the resource type. To do this, either double-click the resource type name or select it and choose Open Picker from the Resource menu. (The command will actually name the resource type. For example, Open ICON Picker.) Then double-click an individual resource, or select it and choose Open Resource Editor from the Resource menu. When an editor is invoked, one or more auxiliary menus may appear, depending on the type of resource you're editing. Some editors, such as the `DITL` editor, allow you to open additional editors for the elements within the resource. The editors vary in their appearance and function, as explained in Chapters 3 and 4.

If you choose Open Using Template from the Resource menu or hold down the Option and Command keys while opening a resource, a list of templates is displayed. You may then select the template that is appropriate for the resource you are opening. For more information on editing with templates, see Chapter 5.

Resource ID numbers

Within a given resource type, resource ID numbers must be unique. Resources can, in general, have any ID number between –32768 and +32767, but you should be aware of the following restrictions which apply to most resources:

- ID numbers from –32768 to –16385 are reserved. Do not use them!
- ID numbers from –16384 to –1 are used for system resources that are owned by other system resources. For example, a dialog box used by a desk accessory (the desk accessory is, itself, a resource of type `DRVR`) would have a number in this range.
- ID numbers from 0 to 127 are used for system resources.
- ID numbers from 128 to 32767 are available to you for your uses.

Some system resources own others. The "owner" contains code that reads the "owned" resource into memory. For example, desk accessories can have their own patterns, strings, and so on. Please see Chapter 5 of *Inside Macintosh,* Volume I, for more information.

Fonts constitute a special case. For information about fonts, see the section on `FONT` resources in Chapter 3.

Chapter 3 **The Bit Editors**

Many important resources on the Macintosh are pictorial. These include cursors, icons, patterns, and fonts. The ResEdit resource editors that handle pictorial resources are discussed in this chapter. Other resource editors are discussed in Chapter 4. For information on templates and resources that are edited via templates, please see Chapter 5.

Overview of the bit editors

Pictorial resource types are edited with a bit or pixel editor. The bit editors in ResEdit 2.1 are all fundamentally alike except for the 'FONT' editor, which is a special case and is discussed separately.

Figure 3-1 shows the layout of a typical bit editor window.

- **Figure 3-1** Bit editor window layout

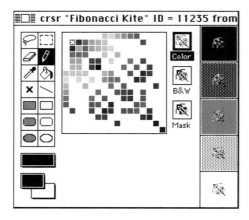

The bit editor window contains these elements:
- A tool palette at the left edge of the window.
- A selector that brings up a tear-off palette of patterns and (in color editors) another pair of selectors, below the tool palette, that allow you to select foreground and background colors. These bring up tear-off color palettes.
- A main editing view that shows an enlarged picture for "fat-bits" editing. The size of this view varies from editor to editor.
- Full-size images of the resource (in monochrome and, when appropriate, in color) and its mask (if it has one), to the right of the main editing window.
- In some of the bit editors, views of the resource on various backgrounds, at the right edge of the window.

When you open a resource that involves color, the editor window is placed on the display with the largest number of colors or gray levels unless you choose otherwise in the Preferences dialog box, shown in Figure 2-9.

Tools

The tools in the palette behave much as they do in familiar paint programs, with the exception of the color-dropper and the pencil. The color-dropper lets you pick up the color of any pixel in the main editing window.

When you are using other drawing tools (for example, the paint bucket), you can access the color-dropper by holding down the Option key. This does not, however, work with the eraser, the marquee, or the lasso.

The square containing the color-dropper is empty when you are editing a black-and-white resource or the mask part or black-and-white image associated with a color resource.

The middle square on the left side of the tool palette is special, and its content changes from editor to editor; in Figure 3-1, which shows the `crsr` editor, it allows you to place the cursor's hotSpot. This is discussed further in the section on cursor editing in this chapter. In some of the editors this square is empty.

When you are editing a colored resource, the pencil tool behaves slightly differently than you might expect if you have edited only in black and white previously. If you click a pixel in the editing view, that pixel changes to the currently selected color. If it is already the currently selected color, it becomes the background color instead.

◆ *Note:* If you try to paste more bits than a resource can hold (for example, if you try to paste a 40- by 40-bit area from a paint program into an `ICON` resource, which can hold only a 32- by 32-bit area), ResEdit pastes the selection centered into the active area, and the boundary of the selection will be outside the active area of the editing window. You can drag to reposition the selection. If a marquee selection is already present in the active area when you perform a paste operation, the `PICT` in the Clipboard is scaled into the selection. You cannot paste into a lasso selection.

If you cut or copy a marquee selection during editing, you can paste it into a file window as a `PICT` resource. The `PICT` resource picker does *not* have to be open when you cut, copy, or paste. When you paste a `PICT` into a color bit editor, the `PICT` is drawn using colors from the resource being edited and the current color palette. If a pasted `PICT` is drawn with odd or unexpected colors, it is because some colors present when the `PICT` was cut or copied are missing from the current color palette. You may want to select a more appropriate color palette and paste again.

Menus

The bit editors have two menus in common: Transform and Color. (Strictly monochrome resources are an exception; their editors do not have a Color menu.) Some of the editors also have individual menus, which are discussed in the sections on those resources.

The Transform menu

The Transform menu is shown in Figure 3-2. It allows you to transform selected regions in several ways. The Flip Horizontal, Flip Vertical, and Rotate commands are familiar from paint programs. The Nudge commands move the selected region by 1 pixel in the indicated direction. (You can also nudge the selected region by using the arrow keys.) The Flip and Rotate commands require a rectangular (marquee) selection.

■ **Figure 3-2** The Transform menu

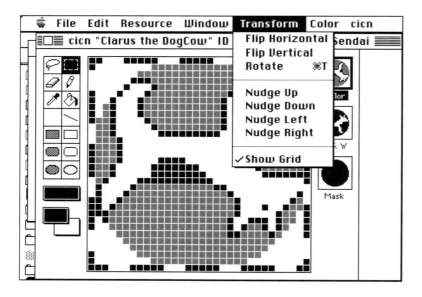

The Color menu

The Color menu is shown in Figure 3-3. It contains a choice of color tables and two other commands. The color table choice determines what appears in the color pop-up menu or tear-off color palette. The choices include the standard set, shown in Figure 3-3 and discussed in this section, as well as any 'clut' resources you have added to the ResEdit Preferences file.

■ **Figure 3-3** The Color menu

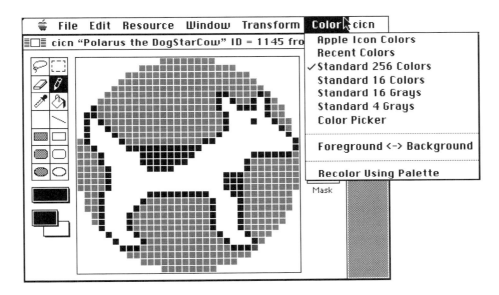

The items on the Color menu include the following:

Apple Icon Colors   Lets you use a palette of Apple's recommended colors for Finder icons.

Recent Colors   Lets you use the set of colors currently present in the resource. These may come from several palettes. This set includes colors that you have selected since the last time you closed the resource but haven't used yet. (When you close a resource, unused colors are automatically removed.)

Standard 256 Colors
Lets you use the standard 8-bit color palette.

Standard 16 Colors
Lets you use the standard 4-bit color palette.

Standard 16 Grays   Lets you use 4 bits of gray levels.

Standard 4 Grays   Lets you use 2 bits of gray levels.

◆ *Note:* If you have custom entries, they appear between Standard 4 Grays and Color Picker.

Color Picker   Lets you use the standard Color Picker, with which you can select any of more than 16 million colors. Try 'em all!

Foreground <-> Background
Swaps foreground and background colors, without affecting the image.

Recolor Using Palette
Merely selecting a palette does not change any of the colors in the resource you're editing. This command recolors the resource using only colors in the current palette.

Palette choices are different for Finder icons. When you are editing 'icl8' or 'ics8' resources, the only color choices available in the Finder icon editor are Apple's recommended icon colors and the standard 256-color (8-bit) palette. For 'icl4' and 'ics4' resources only the standard 16-color (4-bit) palette is available.

◆ *Note:* ResEdit automatically removes any unused colors from a resource when you close it.

If you hold down the Command key and pick a new color, all pixels of the current foreground (or background) color are changed to the new color.

Editing cursors

Cursors are pictorial resources of types 'CURS' (B&W) and 'crsr' (color). Figure 3-4 shows the 'CURS' editor; the 'crsr' editor is shown twice in Figure 3-5. In each of these editors, the middle part of the display has a large image for editing and two smaller full-scale images (three in the case of 'crsr' resources). The upper small image shows the cursor itself. The lower small image is the mask for the cursor, which affects how the cursor appears on various backgrounds. The pixel in the editing window that is marked with an X is the cursor's hotSpot. (The hotSpot is the pixel in the cursor that the Macintosh recognizes as the cursor's location. The hotSpot of the familiar arrow cursor, for example, is its point.) There is a special hotSpot tool on the palette. It is shaped like an X, as you would expect. To place the hotSpot, click this tool and then click anywhere in the main image in the editing window.

Along the right edge of the display, the cursor is drawn to scale on five different background patterns. When the cursor is to be drawn, a hole is first made in the background by turning off the pixels in the area of the screen covered by the mask. Then the cursor is overlaid on the hole. (Figure 3-5 shows a pair of explanatory examples.) Ordinarily, the mask should be just a filled-in outline of the cursor so that the cursor can be seen clearly. To edit the cursor's mask, click the small image labeled Mask. It is then displayed in the editing window. Initially this image is blank; you can drag an upper image to the Mask image to create a mask, or select the mask and paste an image into it.

■ **Figure 3-4** 'CURS' resource editor

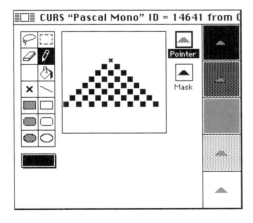

Figure 3-5 shows two almost identical 'crsr' editing windows. These illustrate the difference between *pasting* the black-and-white image (labeled B&W) into the mask (left) and *dragging* the black-and-white image to the mask (right). As you can see, the cursor on the right is entirely opaque: nowhere does the background show through it. The difference is most clearly visible in the Mask images and in the top-right corner images.

■ **Figure 3-5** Color cursor editing: mask examples

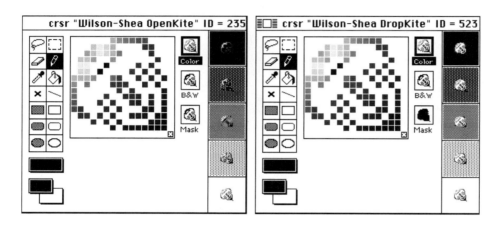

The CURS and crsr menus contain the following command:

Try Pointer   Lets you try out your handiwork by having it become the cursor in use inside ResEdit, in place of the ordinary arrow cursor.

Editing icons

ResEdit contains editors for all the common icon resource types.

Editing `cicn` resources

Ordinary color icons are pictorial resources of type `'cicn'`. Figure 3-6 shows the `'cicn'` editor. Please see the inside front cover for a color illustration of the `'cicn'` editor.

You can transfer images among the three small framed views to the right of the main editing window. These are labeled Color, B&W, and Mask. If you drag across any of these small views, an outline will detach. You can then move that outline to another small view. The destination becomes inverted to indicate that releasing the mouse button will transfer the image. If you transfer the image to the mask, interior bits in the image are set to black.

At the right edge of the editor display are color and black-and-white examples of how the icon looks against the current background.

- **Figure 3-6** Color icon editor

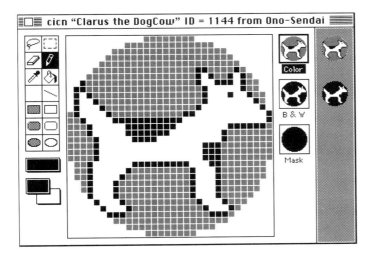

The cicn menu

The cicn menu allows you to choose a background for the display section at the right edge of the window and to bring up a dialog box that lets you set the horizontal and vertical sizes of the icon. These sizes are separate; that is, the icon does not have to be a square. The minimum for both is 8 pixels, and the maximum is 64. The Delete B&W Icon command is active only when the black-and-white icon is selected and is shown in the main editing view.

It is possible to create a 'cicn' resource without a black-and-white image, but because the system uses the image labeled B&W to display the icon on monitors that are set to black and white or to 4 grays or colors, it is probably a good idea to include it.

Creating new color icons

When you create a new 'cicn' resource, you get the last color table you selected. The Color menu, shown in Figure 3-3, lets you choose other color collections. The most commonly used collection is Standard 256 Colors, which lets you pick colors from the 8-bit system color table. Apple recommends that you use colors in the standard 16- and 256-color collections and specifically the Apple Icon Colors, because these are typically present when a 'cicn' icon is drawn.

Finder icons

Finder icons, beginning with system software version 7.0, constitute a suite, or family, of pictorial resources. These include small and large color icons in 16 and 256 colors (types 'ics4' and 'ics8' in the small size, 'icl4' and 'icl8' in the larger size) as well as small and large monochrome icons, now types 'ics#' and the traditional 'ICN#', which is discussed later in this chapter. The large icons are 32-by 32-pixels and effectively share the mask of the 'ICN#' type. The small icons are 16-by 16-pixels; they, too, share a common mask in an 'ics#' resource.

When you use the color-dropper, remember that the color selection is tied to the depth of the image. That is, using the color-dropper to pick up the color of a pixel in, for example, the 'icl4' or 'ics4' image does not change the color selection in the 'icl8' and 'ics8' images (and vice versa), nor does it change the "color" selection (black or white) in the 'ICN#' and 'ics#' images.

Opening any of these resources automatically invokes the Finder™ icon editor and selects the particular resource type for editing, provided Color QuickDraw is present. The 'ICN#' resource type still has its own individual editor but is typically edited in the Finder icon editor with the other members of the suite. (Double-clicking a resource of type 'ICN#' opens the 'ICN#' editor rather than the Finder icon editor if Color QuickDraw is not present, or if you have installed an 'RMAP' resource in the ResEdit Preferences file to override the Finder Icon editor. See Chapter 6 for details.)

Figure 3-7 shows the Finder icon editor during an 'icl8' edit. The other editing windows are quite similar, all of them sharing the tool palette; here, as with the 'cicn' editor, a monochrome illustration cannot fully represent the appearance of a color screen, but the figure should give you some idea of the appearance of this editor. Please see the inside front cover for a color illustration of the Finder icon editor.

- **Figure 3-7** Finder icon family editor

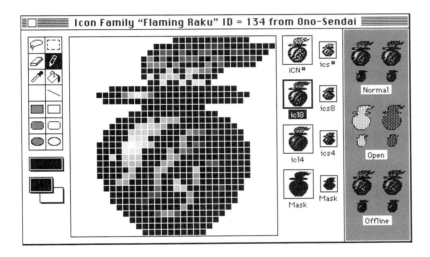

When you click one of the eight small views labeled with resource type names, the corresponding icon is opened for editing. The display bar area on the far right shows the icon in the form of three groups of images against the background that was selected from the Icons menu. The groups are labeled Normal, Open, and Offline. The display shows how the icons are drawn by the system software version 7.0 Finder. In each group, the icon is shown unselected on the left and selected on the right.

The Icon menu

The Icon menu is shown in Figure 3-8. It allows you to select a background for the display section at the right edge of the window; it is useful to be able to check the icon against several different backgrounds. The Delete command allows you to delete the icon type currently being edited. If a mask is being edited, the Delete Resource command allows you to delete the monochrome icon ('ICN#' or 'ics#') that contains the mask.

■ **Figure 3-8** Icon menu

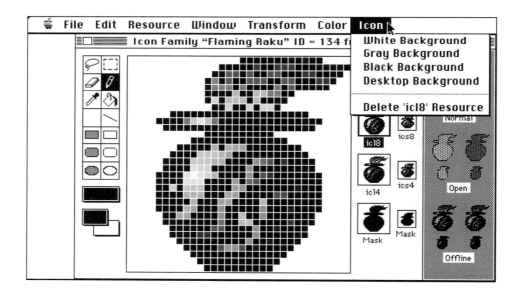

◆ *Note:* Finder Icon family resources that don't exist are drawn in gray, except for masks, which are drawn as black squares. (This allows other family members to appear in the display bar at the right edge of the editor before appropriate masks are created for them.)

`'ICON'` resources

Icons that appear within a program (HyperCard is a good example) are typically resources of type `'ICON'`. The `'ICON'` editor is shown in Figure 3-9. The `'ICON'` resource is relatively simple and consists of a 32- by 32-pixel square, in black and white. It does not have a mask.

■ **Figure 3-9** `'ICON'` resource editor

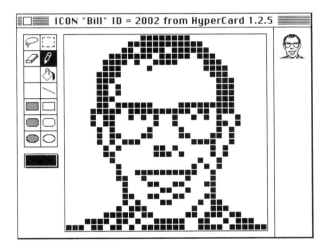

`'ICN#'` resources

The `'ICN#'` resource, part of the Finder Icon suite in system software version 7.0 and later, has long been a common target for ResEdit. The icons that you see on the desktop in system software version 6.0 and earlier, representing applications and their documents, are all `'ICN#'` icons, as are folder icons and even the Trash icon. The `'ICN#'` resource type is edited either in the Finder icon editor, or with its own editor. Both permit you to change any of the pixels in the icon, which are in a 32- by 32-pixel square. When you double-click a resource of type `'ICN#'`, the specific `'ICN#'` editor is ordinarily activated only if Color QuickDraw is not present. If you want to edit a resource of type `'ICN#'` alone and you have Color QuickDraw, you need to generate an `'RMAP'` resource in your ResEdit Preferences file to override the normal operation of ResEdit. See Chapter 6 for details.

The 'ICN#' editor is shown in Figure 3-10.

■ **Figure 3-10** 'ICN#' resource editor

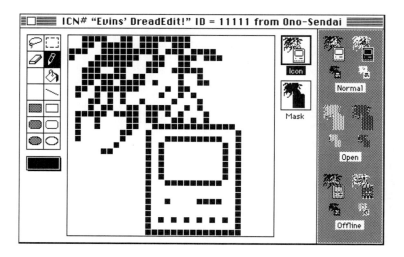

In recent versions of the Finder, 'ICN#' resources are displayed on the screen as follows: First the mask is used to blank an area of the screen. Then an OR operation is performed in the same screen area, using the icon as data. (When a highlighted icon is displayed, the foreground and background "colors"—in this case black and white—are swapped before the OR operation is performed on the data.) If the mask is not the same shape as the outline of the icon, the results will in general be unaesthetic unless the background is black.

List resources

Some pictorial resources contain sets or lists of pictures. Together these pictures make up an individual resource. Editors for list resources have two kinds of editing regions. The first kind is a bit editor, familiar from the editors that have already been described in this chapter. The second kind is used to manipulate the elements in the list.

As with the other bit editors, the picture currently being edited is shown in a box. To edit a different picture, click it in the list on the right. You can drag elements to different positions in the list, and commands on the Edit menu can be used to cut, copy, paste, clear, or duplicate elements when the list is enabled. You can cut or copy list elements only when the list is active. It is possible to paste more than one element at a time. Paste inserts after the currently selected element, or at the end of the list if no element is currently selected. If there are more elements in the list than will fit in the list display area, the scroll bar is enabled.

`'SICN'` resources

The small icon (`'SICN'`) editor is shown in Figure 3-11, with the editing window enabled.

You can add a new small-icon picture by choosing the Insert New SICN command from the Resource menu.

- **Figure 3-11** `'SICN'` resource editor

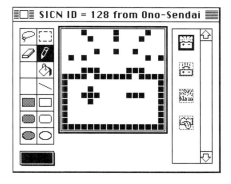

Editing Patterns

ResEdit 2.1 includes editors for four kinds of pattern resources: 'PAT' (black-and-white patterns), 'PAT#' (black-and-white pattern lists), 'ppat' (color patterns), and 'ppt#' (color pattern lists).

Each pattern editor has a menu; the PAT and PAT# menus have only one command, Try Pattern. This command makes your pattern the desktop pattern.

The ppat and ppt# menus have two commands. The Pattern Size command brings up a dialog box, shown in Figure 3-12, that lets you select the size of the basic cell of your pattern. Patterns are replicated or truncated when resized, not scaled. Remember, the black-and-white patterns are always 8-by 8-pixels. Only the color patterns are resized.

The Try Pattern command makes your pattern the desktop pattern. When you are in Try Pattern mode, you can shift back and forth between color and black-and-white versions of the patterns by clicking their respective pictures in the list area (see Figure 3-15 or 3-16).

■ **Figure 3-12** Pattern Size dialog box

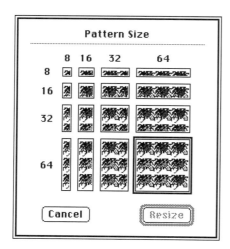

Relative patterns

The `'ppat'` and `'ppt#'` editors support a subset of Relative Patterns. Relative Patterns are used internally by ResEdit in the pattern palette. The editors support 1-bit patterns with no color table entries. These patterns are edited in black and white; the current foreground and background colors replace black and white respectively when the pattern is actually used. For more information, see *Inside Macintosh,* Volume V, page 57.

Custom patterns

You can override the set of patterns provided by ResEdit by installing resources in the ResEdit Preferences file.

To override the patterns available in the black-and-white bit editors, install a `'PAT#'` resource named **Fill Patterns** into the Preferences file. The first pattern in the list is the default choice, and it is a good idea to make this a completely filled (that is, black) pattern.

To override patterns available in the color bit editors, install a `'ppt#'` resource named **Fill Patterns** in the Preferences file. It is a good idea to create relative patterns that adopt the current foreground and background colors. You may also include absolute colors in your patterns. (ResEdit does not permit a single pattern to contain both relative and absolute colors.) When you edit pictorial resource components that are inherently colorless (masks, for example), black-and-white patterns are shown in the bit editor's pattern palette, but internally ResEdit uses the corresponding color patterns. For this reason, you should make the black-and-white version of each pattern a monochrome duplicate of the color pattern.

If you do install your own patterns, you should create similar `'PAT#'` and `'ppt#'` resources for consistency.

`'PAT'` resources

The `'PAT'` resource (black-and-white pattern) editor is shown in Figure 3-13. It displays two panels, with the editing area on the left and the pattern shown on the right. The editing area is small, but it is possible to make some use of the marquee tool.

- **Figure 3-13** `'PAT'` resource editor

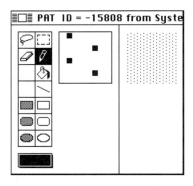

`'PAT#'` resources

The `'PAT#'` resource (black-and-white pattern list) editor is much like the `'SICN'` editor; it is shown in Figure 3-14.

- **Figure 3-14** `'PAT#'` resource editor

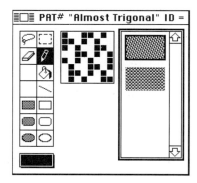

44   ResEdit Reference

`'ppat'` resources

The `'ppat'` resource (color pattern) editor is shown in Figure 3-15.

The black-and-white pattern is limited to 8-by 8-pixels and cannot be resized, although it can be edited. It is displayed on the right edge of the editor window. Unless your color pattern is also 8 pixels square, the black-and-white pattern probably won't look quite like it, as is evident in Figure 3-15.

■ **Figure 3-15** `'ppat'` resource editor

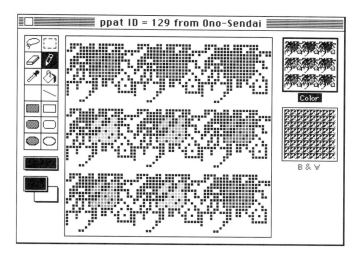

`'ppat'` relative patterns

In the `'ppat'` resource picker, if you hold down the Option key before pulling down the Resource menu, the first item changes to Create New Relative Pattern.

`'ppt#'` resources

The `'ppt#'` resource (color pattern list) editor is shown in Figure 3-16. There are three displays in this editor. The display on the left is a color (or black-and-white) fat-bits version for editing. The display in the middle shows the resulting pattern at full scale, both in color and in black and white. The pattern labeled B&W is sized to match the pattern labeled Color. The display on the right is the list area.

■ **Figure 3-16** `'ppt#'` resource editor

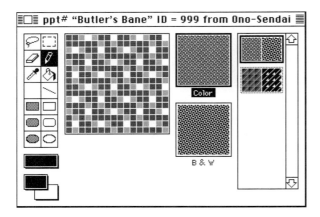

Desktop pattern lists

Desktop patterns, that is, patterns you can select in the general control panel, are found in the `'ppt#'` resource with ID number 0 in the System file. These patterns are restricted to 8-by 8-pixels in size and must contain exactly 8 colors. ResEdit will enforce these restrictions if you edit your System file directly. If you edit `'ppt#'` resource ID 0 from any file other than your System file, ResEdit displays an alert box asking if the resource is a desktop pattern list. You must answer yes if you want to use the resulting patterns in your active System file. If you answer no, any changes you make are likely to cause the number of colors in the pattern to change, and you won't be able to use the result on your desktop. There is no convenient way to create a new desktop pattern list. You should begin with a copy of the `'ppt#'` resource with ID 0 from the System file.

`'ppt#'` relative patterns

If you hold down the Option key before pulling down the Resource menu, the first item changes to Insert Relative Pattern. You cannot insert relative patterns into a desktop pattern list.

`'FONT'` resources

The **Font editor** is a bit editor. It has not been changed from its state in previous versions of ResEdit and will be familiar if you have used ResEdit before; if you need to edit fonts extensively and especially if you need to create new fonts, you should probably use one or more of the excellent third-party utilities that are now available.

The `'FONT'` resource is one of two major ways of representing bitmap (screen) fonts for the Macintosh. (The `'NFNT'` resource, described briefly later in this section, is the other.) The `'FONT'` resource contains a series of pictures that typically represent items in the Macintosh character set, though they need not do so. A chart of the Macintosh character set is presented in Appendix D.

Because the Macintosh displays a character of type on its screen as a bitmap, however, it is possible for the pictures to be just that—pictures. `'FONT'` resources in the Macintosh world can contain scanned images and other pictures just as easily as they can contain the alphabet, numerals, and punctuation marks.

Macintosh computers can modify elements of a font—for example, they can embolden fonts or cause them to slant for an approximation of italics. Print quality on dot-matrix printers (and screen-display accuracy as well) can be improved, however, by providing extra fonts that are constructed with those styles built into them. `'FONT'` resources typically come in families, so that it is possible to display text on the screen (and print it on dot-matrix printers) in several styles, most commonly roman, bold, italic, and a bold-italic combination, without taking processor time to calculate the way such styles should look. These families can also correspond to downloadable PostScript® fonts for laser printers and typesetters.

If you use ResEdit to examine a file of fonts from a recent Macintosh system software version, you will find that it contains three kinds of resources: `'FOND'`, `'FONT'`, and `'vers'` (a record of the version number of the release). The `'FOND'` resource "owns" one or more sizes of a particular font and contains kerning tables and other important information about the `'FONT'` resources it owns. The `'FOND'` resource has a unique ID number, from which the ID numbers of its subsidiary `'FONT'`s are calculated. To find the ID number of a particular `'FONT'` resource, take the ID number of the parent `'FOND'`, multiply by 128, and add the point size of the `'FONT'`. For example, `'FONT'` ID 268 corresponds to New York (family ID 2), in 12 point size.

The ID numbers of `'FOND'` resources may be from 0 (Chicago, the default System font) to 255, inclusive. Apple reserves ID numbers from 0 through 127. Unfortunately, there are a great many bitmap fonts (vastly more, in fact, than 255), so occasional ID number collisions are unavoidable. Version 3.8 and later versions of the Font/DA Mover attempt to resolve such collisions, as do some third-party system-enhancer packages.

There is also another, newer kind of font resource, type `'NFNT'`. Like `'FONT'` resources, `'NFNT'` resources are also owned by `'FOND'` resources. ID numbering of `'NFNT'` fonts is, however, not keyed to the ID number of the parent `'FOND'`. Arbitrary numbering of `'NFNT'` resources helps avoid font ID number collisions and facilitates resolution of conflicts when they do occur. `'NFNT'` fonts, moreover, can contain and display more than 1-bit per pixel and can be assigned absolute colors with a corresponding `'fctb'` resource, which is a color table record. (Font color table records are discussed in *Inside Macintosh*, Volume V, in the section on the Color Manager. The Font Manager is discussed in some detail in *Inside Macintosh*, Volumes IV and V.) ResEdit does not allow you to edit `'NFNT'` fonts, but you can use it to copy and move them. You can also use version 3.8 and later versions of the Font/DA Mover. At least one third-party editor for `'NFNT'` fonts is available.

Editing `'FONT'` resources

Fonts are edited with a bit editor that is a subset of the bit editors for other pictorial resources. This editor has several of the tools you are probably familiar with from such programs as MacPaint®.

The editing window for `'FONT'` resources is divided into four panels: a character-editing panel, a sample text panel, a character-selection panel, and a typical set of graphics tools. These panels are shown in Figure 3-17.

■ **Figure 3-17** `'FONT'` resource editor

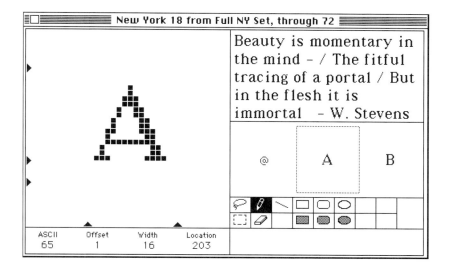

The **character-editing panel,** on the left side of the window, shows an enlargement of the selected character. You can edit it, as with the other bit editors for pictorial resources, by clicking bits on and off with the pencil. Drag the black triangles at the bottom of the character-editing panel to set the left and right bounds of the character (that is, the character width). Two of the three triangles at the left side of the panel control the ascent and descent of characters in the font. If you want to increase the ascent or descent, move the appropriate triangle first. If you put pixels outside the indicated area and then move the triangle, those pixels are wiped out.

▲ **Warning**   Changing the ascent or descent of a character changes the ascent or descent for the entire font. ▲

The third triangle on the left shows the location of the baseline, which is fixed and is displayed only for reference. Below the panel are the character number (labeled ASCII), and the character's offset, width, and location, all in decimal notation.

◆ *Note:* The correspondence between the Macintosh character set number and a real ASCII number is limited. Strictly speaking, ASCII is a set of 128 characters, numbered from 00 ($00, the NULL character) through 127 ($7F, the DEL character), and is intended to represent a basic character set rather than any font or typeface, in a relatively universally understood form. Because the Macintosh character set is oriented toward electronic publishing, which has more (and different) requirements, it has twice as many possible character numbers. (See the section on the 'KCHR' editor later in this chapter.) For ordinary text fonts, characters 0 through 127 of a Macintosh font are the ASCII character set. For Symbol, ITC Zapf Dingbats®, and the various pictorial fonts, however, the correspondence with the ASCII character set is minimal. The Macintosh character set is shown in Appendix D.

The **sample text panel,** at the upper right, displays a sample of text in the font currently being edited. (You can change this text by clicking in the text panel and using normal Macintosh editing techniques.)

The **character-selection panel** is below the text panel. You can select a character to edit by typing it (using the Shift and Option keys if necessary), or by clicking it in the row of three characters shown. To move upward through the character number range, click the right character in the row; to move downward, click the left character. The character you select is boxed in the center of the row. (To scroll quickly, click the right or left character and drag the pointer outside the selection panel, to the right or left.)

The **graphics tools panel**, directly below the character-selection panel, offers several familiar graphics-manipulation tools, including the pencil, eraser, circles, and rectangles. The filled shapes always use a solid black pattern. The 'FONT' editor also includes the marquee tool and the lasso as panel selections.

Any changes you make in the character-editing panel are reflected in the text panel and the character-selection panel, except on monitors displaying more than two colors or gray levels.

You can also change the name of a font. The font name is stored in two places: as the name of the 'FOND' resource of that font family, and as the name of the size 0 'FONT' resource. To change the font name, select the individual 'FOND' resource with the name you wish to change, and choose Get Info from the File menu. To maintain consistency, you should also change the name of the 0 point 'FONT' resource. This resource does not show up in the normal display of all fonts in a file. To display it, hold down the Option key while you open the 'FONT' type from the file window. You will see a generic list of fonts. Select the font with the name you wish to change, and choose Get Info.

Chapter 4 **Other Resource Editors**

Many resources are not of an inherently pictorial nature. ResEdit's editors for these resources and its generalized (hexadecimal) editor are discussed in this chapter. For information on editing template resources, please see Chapter 5.

Using the hexadecimal editor

The hexadecimal resource editor is invoked if you hold down the Option key while opening a resource or choose Open Using Hex Editor from the Resource menu. It is also invoked if you open a resource for which there is no individual editor or template. This editor allows you to edit the resource as hexadecimal or ASCII data. The hex editor can edit resources larger than 255Kb. If a resource is between 256Kb and 511Kb in size, each click in the up or down scroll arrow causes a scroll of two lines; if between 512Kb and 767Kb, each click causes a scroll of three lines; and so on. (The scroll bars keep track of position with an integer, which is a single byte and thus is limited to values between 0 and 255.)

If you enter hexadecimal text when you are using this editor, the editor maintains byte alignment of the incoming data. Thus, if you type 2 into an empty byte, the editor displays 02. If you then type A, the editor displays 2A.

The hex editor has a Search menu. It allows you to search for the occurrence of a pattern in the resource being displayed and allows you to enter the pattern in either hexadecimal or Macintosh character set notation, the latter being loosely described as ASCII, though it is actually considerably larger than the true ASCII set. See Appendix D for a chart of the Macintosh character set. The hex editor also allows you to move to a specified offset from the beginning of the resource you're editing.

'WIND', 'ALRT', and 'DLOG' resources

These three resource types are edited with a tightly interrelated set of editors, so they are considered here as a group.

'WIND' resources display windows on the screen. Figure 4-1 shows the 'WIND' resource editor. At the top of the editing window is a pictorial list of the selectable window styles. Below that is a miniscreen that shows a small picture of the window. You can move and size the window in the miniscreen.

The MiniScreen menu, shown in Figure 4-2, contains a set of screen sizes for you to choose from, and an Other command. It defaults to the dimensions of the Macintosh SE monitor. The Other command lets you add one new size. If you want still more sizes, you can add an appropriate menu to the ResEdit Preferences file.

In Figure 4-1, Custom Color has been selected, and controls that allow you to select colors for various parts of the window are visible. When you choose Custom Color, ResEdit creates a 'actb', 'dctb', or 'wctb' resource that corresponds to the 'WIND', 'ALRT', or 'DLOG' resource you are editing. The first time you change a color, ResEdit reminds you that you are creating a new resource and that if you remove the parent resource you should also remove the extra 'actb', 'dctb', or 'wctb' that is left behind.

'ALRT' and 'DLOG' resources display, respectively, alert and dialog boxes. Editing 'ALRT' and 'DLOG' resources is much like editing 'WIND' resources, except that the corresponding 'DITL' resource is automatically opened if you double-click the picture of the alert or dialog box after opening the resource. (See the next section.) You can select a particular 'DITL' resource to go with a given 'ALRT' or 'DLOG' resource, but the default is one that has the same ID number as the parent resource. 'ALRT' resources have a fixed format, so you cannot select a window type, nor do you have the options of selecting initial visibility or the presence of a close box. 'DLOG' resources do allow these options.

Figure 4-3 shows an 'ALRT' resource open for editing. Just as with the 'WIND' resource example, the editor displays a miniscreen view of the resource.

◆ *Note:* The first item in the 'DITL' associated with any 'ALRT' resource must be a button. The system has no way of telling what is where, so it always regards the first item as a button. Using the Set 'ALRT' Stage Info command from the ALRT menu, you can specify either item 1 or item 2 as the default at any of the four stages of the alert. If item 1 is the default, of course, item 2 need not be a button. By an informal convention in Macintosh programming, item 1 is the OK button and item 2 is the Cancel button if there is a Cancel button. This convention is reflected in the dialog box associated with the Set 'ALRT' Stage Info command.

Figure 4-4 shows a 'DLOG' resource open for editing.

- **Figure 4-1** 'WIND' resource editor

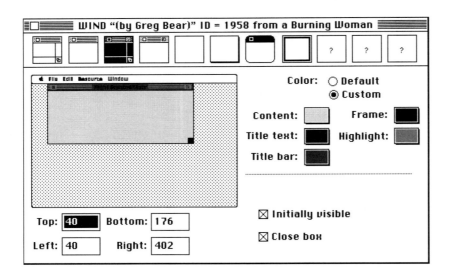

- **Figure 4-2** MiniScreen menu

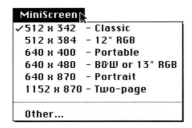

54   ResEdit Reference

■ **Figure 4-3** `'ALRT'` resource editor

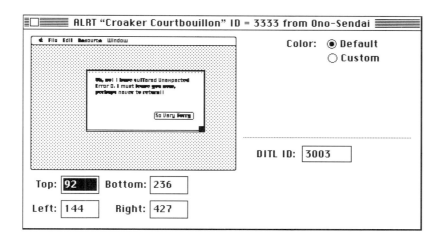

■ **Figure 4-4** `'DLOG'` resource editor

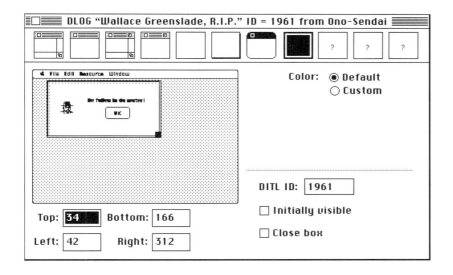

When you display an individual `'WIND'`, `'ALRT'`, or `'DLOG'` resource, a corresponding menu appears. The WIND menu is shown in Figure 4-5, the ALRT menu in Figure 4-7, and the DLOG menu in Figure 4-9. These menus are very similar.

Chapter 4 Other Resource Editors   **55**

They have the following commands in common:

Preview at Full Size
: Displays the resource sized as it is in normal display. Click the mouse to return to the editor.

Auto Position...
: Allows System 7.0 to position the window automatically when it is drawn.

Show Height & Width
: Changes the editable fields at the bottom of the window to show relative size/position information.

Show Bottom & Right
: Changes the editable fields at the bottom of the window to show absolute size/position information.

Use Color Picker
: Lets you use the Color Picker instead of the standard 256-color palette when you set the colors of the various parts of the resource.

■ **Figure 4-5** WIND menu

The WIND menu contains the following commands in addition to those already discussed:

Set 'WIND' Characteristics
: Brings up a dialog box, shown in Figure 4-6, that allows you to title the window and set its refCon and procID. If the procID is not the one associated with any of the pictures at the top of the main window, none of the pictures is selected.

Never Use Custom 'WDEF' for Drawing
> This command defaults to true. It causes the resource to be drawn with the standard 'WDEF' resource from the System file regardless of the value you assign to the procID.

- **Figure 4-6** Setting 'WIND' characteristics

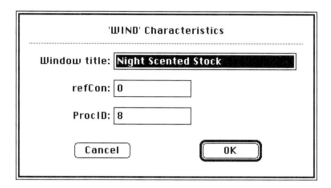

- **Figure 4-7** ALRT menu

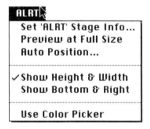

The ALRT menu contains the following command in addition to those already discussed:

Set 'ALRT' Stage Info

    Brings up a dialog box, shown in Figure 4-8, that allows you to set the display conditions for the resource at different stages. You can select how many beeps you want to sound, up to three; whether the OK or Cancel button (actually item 1 or item 2 of the associated 'DITL' resource) is the default; and whether the alert box is to be drawn for each stage. The stages correspond to successive occurrences of the alert condition, although stage 4 is for four or more occurrences. Please see *Inside Macintosh,* Volume I, page 409, for further information.

- **Figure 4-8** 'ALRT' Stage Info dialog box

- **Figure 4-9** DLOG menu

58   ResEdit Reference

The DLOG menu contains the following commands in addition to those already discussed:

Set `'DLOG'` Characteristics
: Brings up a dialog box, shown in Figure 4-10, that allows you to title the window and set its `refCon` and `procID`. If the `procID` is not the one associated with any of the pictures at the top of the main window, none of the pictures is selected.

Never Use Custom `'WDEF'` for Drawing
: This command defaults to true. It causes the resource to be drawn with the standard `'WDEF'` resource from the System file regardless of the value you assign to the `procID`.

■ **Figure 4-10** setting `'DLOG'` characteristics

`'DITL'` resources

The `'DITL'` (dialog item list) resource editor can be invoked directly or from the `'ALRT'` and `'DLOG'` editors. When you first invoke it, it displays an image of the items from the list just as they would be displayed in a dialog or alert box. When you select an item, a dotted rectangle is drawn around it. The rectangle has a size box in its lower-right corner so that you can change its size. If you choose Select All, ResEdit first deselects any selected items, and then selects all items in their order in the item list. You can move an item by dragging it.

The 'DITL' editor uses the Dialog Manager to display 'DITL' resources. This ensures that they look the same when your application displays them as they do in the editor.

Figure 4-11 shows the 'DITL' corresponding to 'DLOG' resource ID 5120 from the Finder. This is the Get Info box.

- **Figure 4-11**   'DITL' resource editor

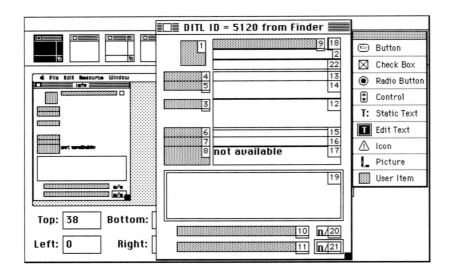

To create a new item, drag the type you want from the item palette. To open an item, either double-click it, or select it and press the Return key.

If you open an item, the item editor, shown in Figure 4-12, is invoked. If you hold down the Option key while opening a 'CNTL', 'ICON', or 'PICT' resource, the hexadecimal editor is invoked. If you hold down the Option and Command keys while opening a 'CNTL', 'ICON', or 'PICT' resource or if you choose the appropriate Open command from the Resource menu, a specific editor for the particular resource is started. Some dialog items are listed as User Items. These are defined in the application, rather than in the Dialog Manager, and are actually built only when you run the application. The item editor has one pop-up menu, which allows you to change the type of the item. Different item types have slightly different editor windows; if another resource (a picture or icon, for example) is referred to by the item, you can select it by ID number. That information takes the place of the Text window in Figure 4-12.

Because they are linked, the 'DITL' resource is usually given the same ID number as the parent 'DLOG' or 'ALRT' resource. This is not necessary, however, and you can assign any 'DITL' resource to any 'ALRT' or 'DLOG' resource.

■ **Figure 4-12** `'DITL'` item editor

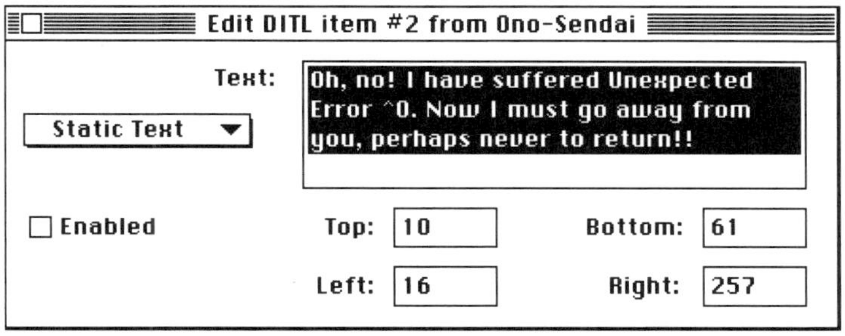

■ **Figure 4-13** DITL menu

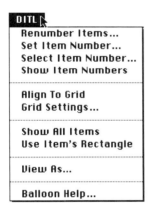

The DITL menu, shown in Figure 4-13, contains the following commands:

Renumber Items
: Allows you to renumber items in the `'DITL'` resource. Remember that item number 1 in a `'DITL'` used by an `'ALRT'` must be a button.

Set Item Number...
: Allows you to specify a new number for a selected item. Some of the items may be renumbered when you do so.

Select Item Number...
: Allows you to select an item by specifying its number. This is useful for items that are obscured by other items or are outside the window. Once you have selected an item, you can open it by pressing the Return key.

Show Item Numbers
: Sets the display to show the number of each item in the `'DITL'` resource. If you hold down the Option key, the current setting of this command is temporarily toggled.

Align To Grid
: Aligns the items on an invisible grid, the size of which defaults to 10 by 10 pixels. If you change the location of an item while Align To Grid is on, the location is adjusted such that the upper-left corner lies on the grid point nearest to the location you gave. If you change an item's size, it is constrained to be a multiple of the current grid setting in each dimension.

Grid Settings...
: Allows you to set the horizontal and vertical grid sizes. These both default to 10 pixels.

Show All Items
: Adjusts the window size so that all items in the item list are visible in the window (or makes the window as large as the current screen size allows, if the screen is smaller). The window size that your program will use when it displays the `'DITL'` is actually stored in the parent `'ALRT'` or `'DLOG'` resource; this command is present solely for your convenience when you are editing the dialog items.

Use Item's Rectangle
: This command is enabled only for `'CNTL'`, `'ICON'`, and `'PICT'` resources. When you choose it, the rectangle specified by the `'DITL'` item, rather than the default rectangle, is used when the `'DITL'` resource is displayed. This is important for pictorial resources in particular, so that the whole picture, rather than some random part of the picture, is shown.

View As...
: Brings up a dialog box, shown in Figure 4-14, that allows you to set the typeface and size in which Edit Text and Static Text items are displayed in the editor. As you can see from the figure, this command does not actually change the resource itself. It is useful if you are designing a dialog box that is to be displayed using a different font from the default font of the editor, which is 12-point Chicago.

Balloon Help...
: Brings up a dialog box with items that relate to Balloon Help in system software release 7.0. There are three types of Balloon Help items; they can be added and deleted with this command. ResEdit always puts Balloon Help items at the end of the item list.

■ **Figure 4-14** DITL menu View As dialog box

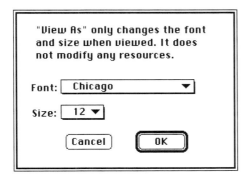

Figure 4-15 shows the Alignment menu. In this illustration, both of the items in the 'DITL' have been selected.

■ **Figure 4-15** Alignment menu

The first six items are enabled only when two or more items are selected. The last two items may pertain to one or more items at a time. Use of all of these items is straightforward.

Any or all of four special items can be used in static text in a 'DITL' item or in a 'STR#' resource. Each is built of a caret (^) followed by a number from 0 to 3. The text of these items can be set by calling the ParamText toolbox procedure. An example of a 'DITL' with these items is shown in Figure 4-16. Please see *Inside Macintosh*, Volume I, page 421, for further information.

■ **Figure 4-16** Special parameter strings

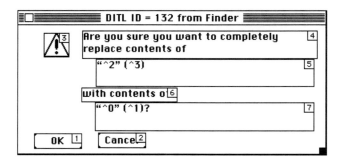

`'BNDL'` resources

To date, `'BNDL'` resources have been mysterious, opaque, and difficult to learn about.

They are associated historically with a fairly complex set of concepts, but in fact their only function is to bring together an application's documents (including the application file itself) and their icons for the Finder. Any application that has a distinct icon on the desktop also contains a `'BNDL'` resource. For more details on the structure and concept of the `'BNDL'` resource, please refer to Appendix C, "The `'BNDL'` Resource."

The `'BNDL'` editor in ResEdit 2.1 helps you create a bundle consisting of the necessary `'BNDL'`, `'FREF'`, and Finder icon resources and saves you the trouble of dealing with the internal workings of the bundle concept. The basic view you get when you first bring up the `'BNDL'` editor is shown in Figure 4-17. (The extended view is shown in Figure 4-19.)

■ **Figure 4-17** `'BNDL'` resource editor, simple view

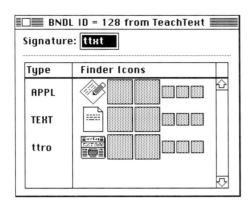

The Finder bundles together documents, applications, and their icons with a four-character signature, which must be unique for every application. All the necessary resources to do this are stored in the so-called Desktop file (or in the desktop database in system software version 7.0). This signature is shown in the first line of the window. All characters in the Macintosh character set (see Appendix D) are allowed in the signature. To register a unique signature for your own application, please contact Macintosh Developer Technical Support at Apple Computer, Inc.

This signature is used as the creator code for all files that are part of the bundle (the creator code is a property of every file and can be set using the Get File/Folder Info command on the File menu). Every file on the Macintosh also has a file type, which is another four-character field (several standard file types are defined: APPL for application, TEXT for plain text document, PICT for picture files, and so on). This file type is used not only to differentiate among different kinds of files but also to associate distinct icons with different files having the same creator (that is, those that belong to the same application). This is what the list in the bottom part of the `'BNDL'` editor window does. To create a new file type and its icon, choose Create New File Type from the Resource menu. Enter the file type in the left column and open the Finder Icon field in the right column by selecting Choose Icon from the BNDL menu or by double-clicking the field.

Figure 4-18 shows the Icon chooser. Here you can either select an existing icon for your file type, or you can create your own by pressing the New button. Note that even though the `'BNDL'` editor shows the entire Finder icon family, because of screen real estate considerations you will see only a list of `'ICN#'` resources in this window. Versions of the Finder before system software release 7.0 use only `'ICN#'` icons.

■ **Figure 4-18** The Icon chooser

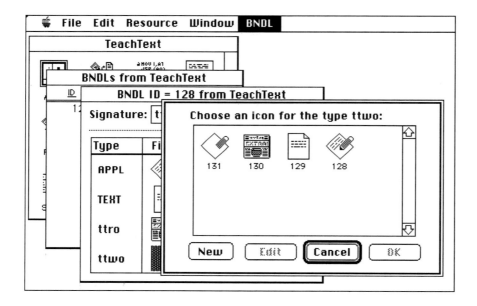

Once you have associated all your file types with distinct icons (remember to include the file type APPL for your application itself), you need take only a few more steps to make the Finder display your icons.

Choose either the Get File/Folder Info command or the Get Info for This File command from the File menu, and select your application from the resulting list of files. Now set the file type to APPL and the creator to the signature you have entered in the 'BNDL' resource. Then set the Bundle bit and clear the Inited bit. This tells the Finder that your application contains a 'BNDL' resource and that it hasn't already seen your file. If the Finder doesn't immediately show your new icon, select your application and use the Get Info command in the Finder.

◆ *Note:* Once the Finder has seen your 'BNDL' resource and loaded the icons into its Desktop file, it will never again look at your 'BNDL', even if you clear the Inited bit. In order to change the 'BNDL' resource or to change some icons, you must either remove your 'BNDL' resource from the Desktop file manually using ResEdit (this works, but is not recommended) or recreate the Desktop file. To do this, hold down the Option and Command keys while restarting your Macintosh computer. The Finder will then ask you if you want to rebuild the Desktop file. Remember that when you do this, you lose all comments you may have entered in the Get Info windows in the Finder in system software previous to system software version 7.0.

If you want to move information from one file type to another within the `BNDL` resource you can do so by using the commands on the Edit menu. For copying operations, all necessary information (including the Finder icons) is copied with the file type. If you clear or cut a file type in the `BNDL` resource, please note that for safety reasons the Finder icons are not removed (because good icons are hard to design, it is generally considered better to waste a few bytes than to delete one accidentally).

If you ever need to tinker with the internal workings of the `BNDL` resource, you can edit all information stored in the `BNDL` and associated `FREF` resources by choosing Extended View from the BNDL menu. See Figure 4-19.

■ **Figure 4-19** `BNDL` resource editor, extended view

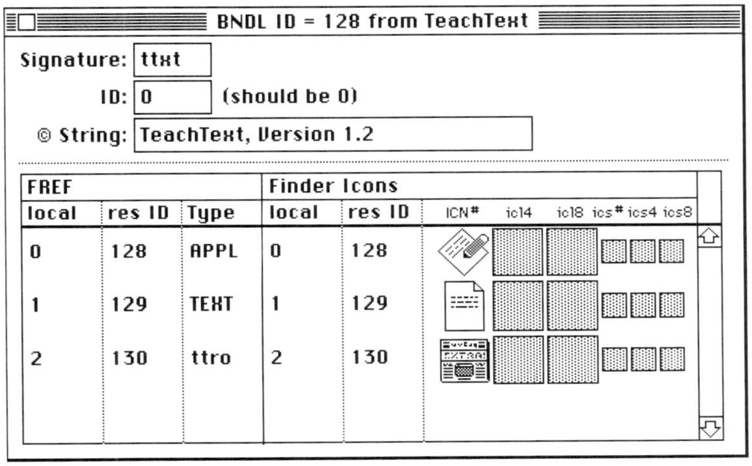

For historical reasons the third line of the extended view, which displays the contents of the signature resource, is labeled © String. This is because before the introduction of the `vers` resource to keep track of version information, the signature resource was used to store such information. Today the Finder ignores the contents of the signature resource unless the `vers` resources are missing. In that case the Finder displays the contents in its Get Info window. The `vers` resource and its editor are described in detail in this chapter.

'clut' and 'pltt' resources

The 'clut' (color look-up table) and 'pltt' (palette) resources are used to store color and gray-scale information. They are largely interchangeable, but the 'pltt' resource type contains usage information in addition to the information contained in a corresponding 'clut' resource. Palettes are associated with windows. For more information, see the Palette Manager and Color Manager chapters in *Inside Macintosh*, Volume V. ResEdit 2.1 includes an editor for 'clut' and 'pltt' resources, shown in its 'clut' version in Figure 4-20.

■ **Figure 4-20** 'clut' resource editor

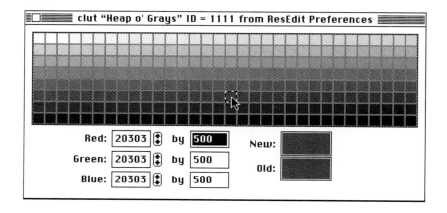

If you click any color patch, the editor draws a marquee around it to indicate that it is selected. Shift-click to make an extended selection. When a single color patch is selected, you can change its value by typing new numbers into the boxes labeled Red, Green, and Blue at the bottom of the editing window, or by clicking the up or down arrows.

The arrows change the indicated value by the amount shown but cannot create a value that is greater than 65535 or less than 0. For example, if the change size is set to 500 and you attempt to decrease a value that is already less than 500 by clicking the corresponding down arrow, the value is set to 0. The default change size is 500, as shown in Figure 4-20.

To create a new color patch, choose Insert New Color from the Resource menu or press Command-K. To remove a color patch you must use Cut or Clear, because the Delete key changes only the contents of the labeled boxes.

■ **Figure 4-21** clut menu

The clut menu, shown in Figure 4-21, contains the following commands:

Blend   Generates a ramp, or blend, between the endpoints of a selected range of colors. If only three color patches are selected, the middle color will be set to a value halfway between the extremes. If fewer than three color patches are selected, this command is dimmed and cannot be used.

Complement   Changes the values of selected colors to the values of their complements.

Load Colors...   Brings up a dialog box that allows you to load colors and gray levels from the available palettes and color look-up tables. These include the standard 8-bit (256-color) set, the standard 4-bit set, black-and-white, Apple's recommended colors for icons, and any others that are available in the ResEdit Preferences file or in any other files you have open. Using this command replaces the current colors with the new ones.

RGB Model
CMY Model
HSB Model
HLS Model   These commands allow you to select from one of four models for handling colors. The models are:

> RGB: Red/Green/Blue
> CMY: Cyan/Magenta/Yellow
> HSB: Hue/Saturation/Brightness
> HLS: Hue/Lightness/Saturation

RGB is the default model.

The pltt menu is identical to the clut menu except that it includes a Usage command that brings up a dialog box in which you can specify usage information for the particular `pltt` resource.

The Sort menu (not shown) allows you to sort by any of the three criteria of the current model. That is, if you are using the RGB model, it lets you sort by amount of red, green, or blue.

The Background menu (not shown) lets you choose white, gray, or black as the background color of the area of the editing window having no color patches, including the border around the patches.

'INTL', 'it10', and 'it11' resources

The 'INTL' resource combines the functionality of the 'it10' and 'it11' resources. That is, 'INTL' "US" ID = 0 is the same as 'it10' "US" ID = 0, and 'INTL' "US" ID = 1 is the same as 'it11' "US" ID = 0. These resources are used in international localization. For further information, see *Inside Macintosh,* Volume V, Chapter 16. Each of these resources (whether you edit them as 'INTL' or as 'it10' and 'it11') is shown as a window with a set of boxes to be filled in and some buttons that can be clicked. Figures 4-22 and 4-23 show the windows for 'it10' and 'it11' resources.

■ **Figure 4-22** Editing an 'it10' resource

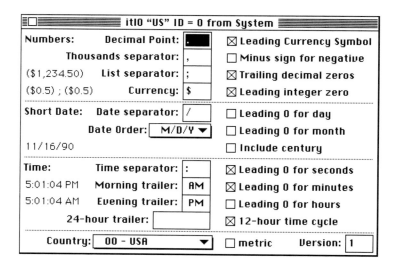

■ **Figure 4-23** Editing an `itl1` resource

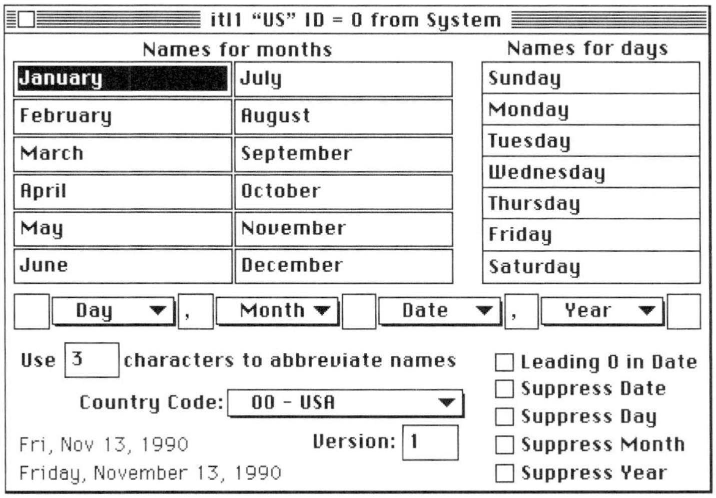

`KCHR` resources

The `KCHR` resource controls keyboard mapping. The main `KCHR` editing screen is shown in Figure 4-24, with the Command and Shift keys pressed; the dead-key editor is shown in Figure 4-25. Appendix A contains an in-depth discussion of the `KCHR` resource itself, and a short section of `KCHR` questions and answers appears in Chapter 6.

■ **Figure 4-24** Editing a 'KCHR' resource

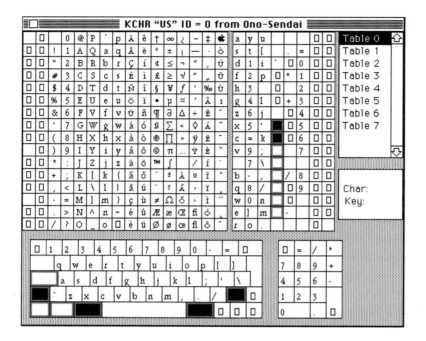

The main 'KCHR' editor

The display for the main 'KCHR' editor (Figure 4-24) is divided into five parts, which are described in the sections that follow.

The character chart

The character chart is the large rectangle at the upper-left corner of the display.

This chart shows the 256 characters that make up the currently selected font. It displays the character generated by the currently pressed key, by highlighting it. You can also display a character by clicking with the mouse in either the keyboard region or the virtual keycode chart. These characters can be assigned to keys on the keyboard. To assign a character to a key, drag the character either to a keycap in the keyboard region or to the virtual keycode chart. You cannot assign characters to the Command, Option, Shift, Caps Lock, Control, Return, or Enter keys.

The table chart

The table chart is at the upper-right corner of the display.

The Shift, Caps Lock, Option, Command, and Control keys are considered to be *modifiers*. No combination of modifier keys generates a character code unless some other key is also pressed. The table chart shows which table is used by the currently depressed modifier key combination.

Please note that although there are 256 possible combinations of modifier keys, most versions of the `KCHR` resource use only 8 tables, and very few ever use more than 16. This is because similar modifier key combinations are frequently mapped to the same table. For example, in the U.S. `KCHR` resource, all combinations involving the Control key point to Table 6. Also, the Caps Lock and Shift combination points to Table 1 (which is pointed to by the Shift key) rather than Table 2 (which is pointed to by the Caps Lock key on its own).

To change the table used by a modifier key combination, press that combination of modifier keys and click a different table. The mapping is changed by the editor. This feature is probably of very little use, and the information is included here for completeness. Here is a listing of the tables as they are pointed to by various modifier key combinations in the U.S. `KCHR`, as supplied:

- Table 0 is shown when none of the modifier keys is pressed, or when the Command key or Command and Shift keys are pressed.
- Table 1 is shown when the Shift key or Caps Lock and Shift keys are pressed.
- Table 2 is shown when the Caps Lock key is pressed.
- Table 3 is shown when the Option key is pressed.
- Table 4 is shown when the Shift and Option keys are pressed.
- Table 5 is shown when the Caps Lock and Option keys are pressed.
- Table 6 is shown when the Option and Command keys are pressed.
- Table 7 is shown when the Control key (and any other keys) are pressed.

The virtual keycode chart

The virtual keycode chart is at the top of the display, slightly to the right of center.

This chart shows all 128 keycodes in the current table and highlights the keycode that is generated if you press a particular key with the current modifier key combination. These keycodes come from the keyboard and are virtual in the sense that further translation has to take place before a Macintosh character set number results and a character can be displayed.

The keyboard region

The keyboard region occupies the bottom of the display, below the character chart and the virtual keycode chart.

This area reflects a particular keyboard layout. You can choose a different keyboard for displaying the virtual keycodes by using the View As command on the KCHR menu. The Apple® Extended Keyboard and Extended Keyboard II have two sets of modifier keys, and you can use the Uncouple Modifier Keys command, also on the KCHR menu, to get access to the alternate modifier keys (the ones on the right side of the keyboard, which are usually coupled with the ones on the left side). If you do not have the Apple Extended Keyboard or Extended Keyboard II connected to your Macintosh, you cannot choose the Uncouple Modifier Keys command.

Note that the modifier keys shown in the keyboard picture have a gray border. This border has two purposes:

- It reminds you that you cannot drag a character from the character chart onto a modifier key.
- It helps you find the modifier keys in the virtual keycode chart. (They have a gray border there, too.)

Note also that if you press the Option key, some keys in the display are shown with solid black borders. These are "dead" keys. If you click a dead key, the special editor for dead keys is invoked. For more information on editing dead keys, see "Editing Dead Keys," later in this chapter.

The information region

The information region is at the right edge of the display, below the table chart.

This small box shows you the current character code and virtual keycode (if there are any), both in hexadecimal form.

Editing dead keys

Some combinations of keys do not immediately specify a character. Because nothing appears on the screen and the cursor does not move when these combinations are pressed, they are called dead keys. They act to modify the next key that is pressed after the dead key is released. The special editor for dead keys is shown in Figure 4-25.

■ **Figure 4-25** Editing a dead key

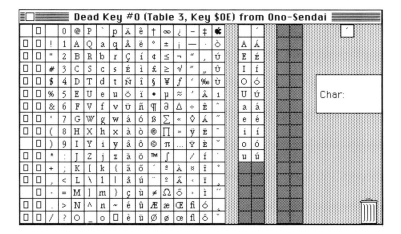

The dead-key editor

The display for the dead-key editor is divided into five functional sections.

The character chart

The character chart is on the left side of the editing window.

This chart displays the character codes and is used to assign a different character code to either a completion character, a substitution character, or the nomatch character; you assign a code by dragging the character to its new location. If you drag a character to one of the empty slots (displayed in gray) in the completion and substitution character pair list, you automatically add a new pair.

The nomatch character

If the character typed after the dead key doesn't fit, a nomatch character is displayed, followed by the character you have typed. For example, Option-E must be followed by a vowel; it doesn't make much sense to put an accent mark on a *k*. The nomatch character for the current dead key is shown in the upper-right corner of the window.

The completion and substitution character pair list

The completion and substitution pair list is just to the right of the character chart.

This list shows the translation rules for the dead key that is currently selected. There are two columns, allowing for a total of 32 dead keys. The left half of each column shows all completion characters; the right half shows all substitution characters. If the character typed after the dead key is one of the completion characters, the matching substitution character is actually produced. For example, pressing Option-e and then e produces the character é.

The Trash

To remove a completion/substitution character pair, just drag either character from that pair in the completion/substitution pair list to the Trash icon in the lower-right corner of the window.

The information region

The information region is on the right edge of the window, and contains the word *Char:*.

This area contains the character code in hexadecimal form whenever you click one of the other parts of the editor.

The menus

The 'KCHR' editor has three menus: KCHR, Font, and Size.

The KCHR menu

This menu is shown in Figure 4-26.

■ **Figure 4-26** The KCHR menu

The KCHR menu contains the following commands:

View As...   If you have the Key Layout file (which has been part of the system software since version 4.2) in your System Folder, you'll be presented with a list of keyboards to be used for displaying the virtual keycodes. Note that you are *not* changing the layout of a particular keyboard, but the 'KCHR' resource that is used by *all* keyboards and is based on the ISO (International Standards Organization) Apple Desktop Bus™ (ADB) keyboard.

Uncouple Modifier Keys
  This command is enabled when you have an ADB extended keyboard connected to your computer. It can be used to uncouple the right modifier keys (see the note immediately following) and thus edit the tables used by them. Please note that the 'KCHR' editor automatically recouples them whenever you bring another window to the front or close the editor.

Chapter 4   Other Resource Editors   77

◆ *Note:* When you choose the Uncouple Modifier Keys command, you must also use the View As command to set the current keyboard to a keyboard that supports uncoupled modifier keys. To avoid confusion, and because not all keyboards support this decoupling, it is recommended that you not make use of this command.

New Table   Creates a new empty table.

Duplicate Table   Creates an identical copy of the current table.

Remove Unused Tables
                    Looks for tables that are not used by any modifer key combination, and removes them.

Remove Duplicate Tables
                    Checks for tables that are identical, reassigns modifier key combinations as necessary to one table, and removes any duplicates.

Edit Dead Key...   Displays a dialog box (see Figure 4-27) containing a list of all dead keys and lets you select one to edit. Note that there is a shortcut to edit dead keys: You can either click a dead key on the screen, or press the dead key on the keyboard. In either case the dead-key editor will automatically appear.

Convert To Dead Key
                    Whenever you hold down a key with any combination of modifier keys and choose this menu command, the key will be converted to a dead key. You can then use the Edit dead key command to define all valid completion and substitution characters for the new dead key.

Remove Dead Key   This command is enabled only when a dead-key window is open. It removes the dead key currently being edited from the dead-key list, converting it into a live key in the process.

■ **Figure 4-27** Dead Key Edit Dialog Box

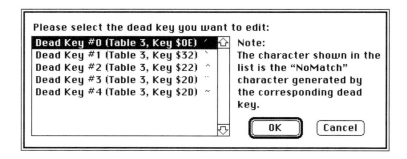

The Font menu

This menu lets you choose a font for displaying the characters in the editor's window.

The Size menu

This menu lets you choose a size for the characters displayed in the editor's window. All characters in the window are automatically resized.

◆ *Note:* If you are editing `'KCHR'` resources on a Macintosh SE, Macintosh Plus, or Macintosh 512K enhanced, the `'KCHR'` editor automatically sets the size to 9 points so that the editing window fits on the screen.

`'MENU'` resources

Menus are an important part of the Macintosh user interface and are found in all applications and many desk accessories. They are stored in resources of types `'MENU'` (regular menus), 'cmnu' (MacApp® temporary menus; these are converted into `'MENU'` resources by PostRez during the MacApp build process, so you will never find one in an application), `'CMNU'` (MacApp permanent menus; these will be supported in future versions of MacApp), and `'mctb'` (menu color tables for any of the preceding types). The `'cmnu'` and `'CMNU'` types differ from regular menus in that they have an additional command number field stored for each item in the menu. ResEdit 2.1 supports editing of all these menu resource types with a new editor that automatically integrates the color information stored in the `'mctb'` resources and thereby allows editing of menus in color. See the inside front cover for a color illustration of menu editing.

The display of the menu editor, shown in Figure 4-28, is divided into two sections. The left side shows the entire menu, and the right side displays detailed information about the item selected on the left side. To accommodate menus with many items, the box on the left side has a scroll bar.

■ **Figure 4-28** 'MENU' resource editor

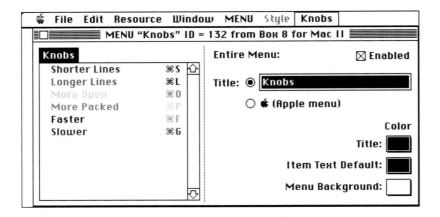

If the title of the menu is selected, the editor not only allows you to change the title but also displays some information about the entire menu. You can enable or disable the entire menu and also select colors for the menu's title, for the item text default, and for the menu background. On machines capable of displaying color, the color patches are pop-up menus that let you choose a color from a palette corresponding to the pixel-depth of the deepest device intersecting the window. Should you want or need to enter a color in RGB values, you can choose Use Color Picker from the MENU menu and set the color using the standard color picker. On monochrome machines the color picker is opened whenever you click the color patch, because a palette cannot be displayed adequately. Since the Apple character can't easily be generated on some keyboards, there is also a convenient radio button to make the menu title the Apple character instead of text entered in the box. If you do enter the Apple character, the editor automatically selects the radio button. In some typefaces there are two Apple characters, only one of which causes the editor to select the radio button. You can enter it by typing Control-T. The other Apple is Option-Shift-K.

When you create a new menu, there are no items to select in order to start the editing process. You can choose Create New Item from the Resource menu, type Command-K, or press the Return key.

When you choose an individual menu item, the display changes to the one shown in Figure 4-29. You can either edit the text of the item directly or you can use the radio button to make the item a separation line (which you can also do by entering a hyphen in the text box). You can use the Style menu to select a different style (bold, italic, and so on) for each item, and you can enable or disable the item with the checkbox in the upper-right corner. For each item you can assign a Command-key equivalent (the Menu Manager is not case sensitive, so for esthetic reasons and consistency you should use only uppercase characters) and an item mark, which you can choose from an extensible pop-up menu shown in Figure 4-30. Both the Command-key equivalent and the Mark character can be displayed in color. If you want to do that, select a color from the corresponding color palette pop-up menus.

- **Figure 4-29** 'MENU' line item edit

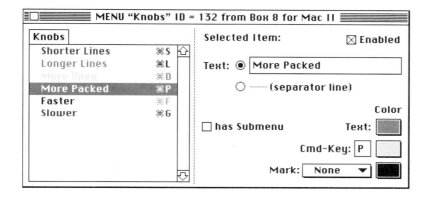

- **Figure 4-30** 'MENU' Mark pop-up menu

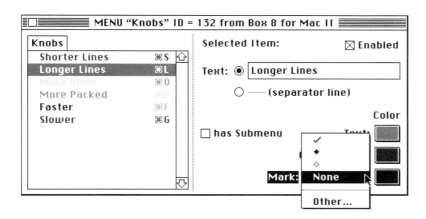

To make an important item look unique, you can put an icon in front of the item's text. Use the Choose Icon command from the MENU menu to get the dialog box shown in Figure 4-31.

■ **Figure 4-31** 'MENU' Icon Chooser dialog box

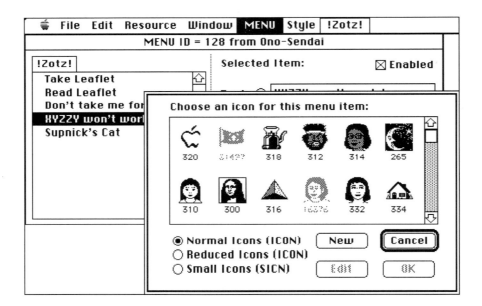

Because of Menu Manager restrictions, the icon's ID must be in the range of 257 to 511 in order for it to be used in a menu. All other icons are displayed in gray. If a regular item seems to be too large for your menu, you can select the Reduced Icons (ICON) radio button to shrink the icon to a more convenient 16- by 16-pixel size or you can add a small icon (resource type 'SICN') instead of a regular one. If you later want to remove the icon from an item, choose Remove Icon from the MENU menu. So that the window will not appear cluttered, the menu on the left side of the editing window does not show icons.

If you want to see how your menu looks in real life, you can try it out at the right edge of the menu bar. Its title is outlined with a black border to show you that this is not a regular menu but a sample of the menu you are editing.

Sometimes a menu may become overcrowded with items. That's when you should start to think about organizing the items in groups and making the menu hierarchical. The menu editor helps you create submenus by providing you with the option to turn any item into a submenu just by clicking a checkbox. To edit the items of the submenu, either choose Open Submenu from the Resource menu or double-click on the item's text.

If you happen to edit a `'cmnu'` or `'CMNU'` resource for inclusion in a MacApp program, you will notice that an additional field in the item's display lets you set the command number for each item. This is shown in Figure 4-32, just to the right of center.

■ **Figure 4-32** Editing a `'cmnu'` resource

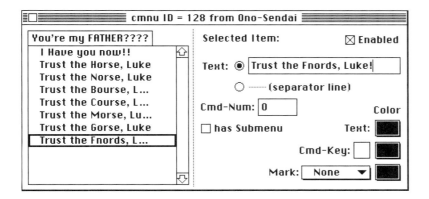

The menu editor also lets you rearrange the items in your menu. You can either use the standard commands on the Edit menu, or you can put an item in a new position by dragging it around in the menu on the left side of the window. As you move the item around, a black line between items shows you where the item will move if you release the mouse button.

Selecting colors from the various pop-up palettes actually modifies an `'mctb'` resource (menu color table), which is transparently generated and changed for you. If you want to get rid of the colors you have set, you can reset the `'mctb'` resource by choosing Use Default Colors from the MENU menu.

The `'MENU'` resource has two assigned ID numbers. One of these is the resource ID number; it is set by getting information on the resource from the picker window or the editor window. This is the ID number that always appears in the picker window. The other is the menu ID number; it is set inside the editor and is returned by the Menu Manager of the Macintosh toolbox in response to MenuSelect and MenuKey calls. Keeping these two numbers the same, while not required, avoids confusion, and in fact they default to the same number. See Chapter 6 for more information.

The corresponding `'MDEF'` ID number is almost always 0. This refers to the standard `'MDEF'` in the System file, which is generally appropriate. Some menus (palettes, for example) do, however, need to be drawn differently. These could use separate `'MDEF'` resources and hence would not have 0 in this field. Figure 4-33 shows the `'MENU'` and `'MDEF'` ID number dialog box.

■ **Figure 4-33** 'MENU' ID dialog box

'TEXT' and 'styl' resources

When styled text is copied to the clipboard or stored in a resource file by applications, the style information pertaining to the text and the text itself are stored in two resources, one of type 'TEXT', and one of type 'styl'. Previous versions of ResEdit have allowed template editing of the 'TEXT' resource, but have not allowed access to 'styl' information. The 'TEXT'/'styl' editor, shown in Figure 4-34, has menus for Font, Size, and Style, and works much as you would expect a text editor to.

■ **Figure 4-34** 'TEXT' and 'styl' editor

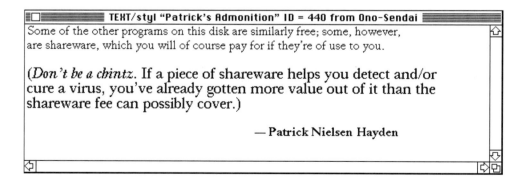

If you attempt to open a `'styl'` resource, the editor is invoked with the associated `'TEXT'` resource. A `'styl'` resource doesn't make much sense without some text to which it can be applied.

`'vers'` resources

The `'vers'` resource is typically part of a Macintosh application but can be found in any file. It is defined as a general source of version information, but currently displays its information in the Get Info window displayed by the Finder.

The `'vers'` editor is shown in Figure 4-35. The "Version number" is displayed in three parts, with a fourth "Non-release" part below. The allowable ranges for these numbers are as follows: main number: 0–99; second part: 0–9; third part: 0–9; fourth part: 0–255. The editor will reject numbers outside the allowable ranges, even though it appears to accept and save them; if you close and reopen the resource, they show up as 0. If your version number has letters in it, you should put the letters only in the short and long version strings. The Release and Country Code items are pop-up menus. Release allows you to select from Development, Alpha, Beta, and Final; Country Code is a longer list, currently containing 54 countries. The short version string should, in general, contain only the ordinary version number (for example, 2.1a5); the long version string can also include copyright notices, authors' names, release dates, and other relevant information. It is displayed in the Get Info window.

■ **Figure 4-35** Editing a `'vers'` resource

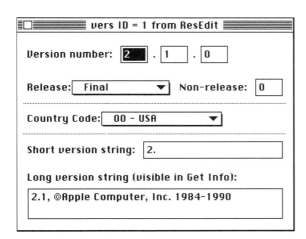

Chapter 5 **ResEdit Templates**

One generic way of editing a resource is to fill in the fields of a dialog box. The contents of the dialog box are specified by a template contained, typically, in ResEdit's own resource fork or in the ResEdit Preferences file. This chapter discusses template editing and tells you how to create your own templates.

Template characteristics

If you open an actual resource of any of the types listed in this chapter, you will find yourself editing in a dialog box, the contents of which are specified by the template of the same name as that resource type. (For example, the 'LAYO' resource, discussed further in Chapter 6, is controlled by the 'TMPL' resource named LAYO in ResEdit.) The template specifies the format of the resource and also specifies what labels should be put beside the editText items in the dialog box used for editing the resource.

◆ *Note:* A template can contain a maximum of 2048 fields. For the purpose of enumerating, a field is defined as any item that is drawn on the screen. That is, a label counts as a field, as does a separator, and so on. This limiting number of 2048 is reached rather easily, particularly in resources with repeating lists, as for example, 'pltt'.

The 'TMPL' resource inside ResEdit is recursive, in the sense that the contents of each of these named 'TMPL' resources is itself a template. (There is even, of course, one for 'TMPL' itself.) As of late 1990, ResEdit contains 'TMPL' resources for these resource types:

'actb'	'acur'	'ALRT'	'APPL'	'BNDL'	'cctb'
'clut'	'CMDK'	'CMNU'	'cmnu'	'CNTL'	'CTY#'
'dctb'	'DITL'	'DLOG'	'DRVR'	'FBTN'	'fctb'
'FDIR'	'finf'	'fld#'	'FOND'	'FONT'	'FREF'
'FRSV'	'fval'	'FWID'	'GNRL'	'hwin'	'icmt'
'inbb'	'indm'	'infa'	'infs'	'inpk'	'inra'
'insc'	'itlb'	'itlc'	'itlk'	'LAYO'	'MBAR'
'mcky'	'mctb'	'MENU'	'nrct'	'PAPA'	'PICK'
'PICT'	'pltt'	'POST'	'ppat'	'PRC0'	'PRC3'
'PSAP'	'qrsc'	'resf'	'RMAP'	'ROv#'	'RVEW'
'scrn'	'SIGN'	'SIZE'	'STR '	'STR#'	'TEXT'
'TMPL'	'TOOL'	'vers'	'wctb'	'WIND'	'wstr'

Editing

When you are editing a template, the Tab key moves you forward from field to field within the template. Shift-Tab moves you backward. Here, however, the term *field* means an active area with an editable value in it. Fields are shown on the screen as boxes.

To add a new field to a repeating sequence in a template, select a separator, which is usually a set of asterisks (*****), and choose Create New Field from the Resource menu.

Some templates control windows or resources that contain rectangles. Some of these templates will have a Set button that lets you draw a rectangle on the screen to delimit the resource. The pixel numbers for the rectangle are automatically copied to the appropriate fields in the template. There is a Set button in the `LAYO` template, which is discussed in Chapter 6; another is shown in Figure 5-1.

Values can be entered into numeric fields in either decimal or hexadecimal notation. You can enter a hexadecimal number into any numeric field by preceding it with a dollar sign ($).

`PICT` editing

There is a custom editor for `PICT` resources, but it only displays the resources at full size, and does not permit you to alter them. You can edit `PICT` resources with the template that exists for them, which is shown in Figure 5-1, by choosing Open Using Template from the Resource menu. If you click the Set button, you can then draw a rectangle on the screen to define the size of the picture frame that is used when the resource is displayed. Otherwise, you can define the size of the frame by entering values in the fields as you would in any template.

■ **Figure 5-1** The template editor for 'PICT'

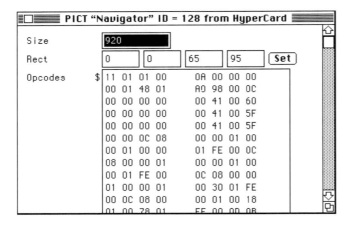

For other examples of template editing, see the description of the 'STR#' resource template in this chapter and the description of the 'LAYO' resource in Chapter 6.

Creating new templates

You can generate templates for your own resource types. These templates, which are resources of type 'TMPL', need not reside within ResEdit. The ResEdit Preferences file in the System Folder is a good place to keep them.

Template example

The `'TMPL'` resource inside ResEdit with name STR# is shown in Figure 5-2. It is shown here as a ready example of what `'TMPL'` innards look like on the screen.

- **Figure 5-2**   `'TMPL'` definition for type `'STR#'`

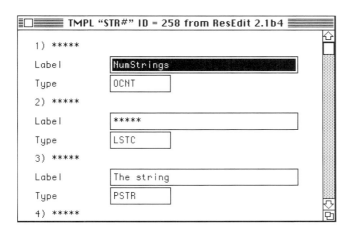

Figure 5-3 shows the same template being used to edit an actual `'STR#'` resource. You can see the correspondence between the items in the `'TMPL'` resource and the resulting display.

- **Figure 5-3**   `'STR#'` template in use

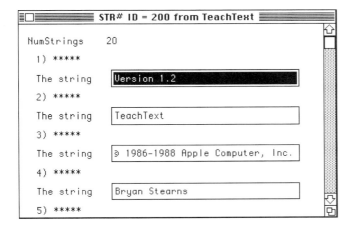

You can look through the other templates and compare them with the structures of their corresponding resources to get a feel for how you might define your own resource template. (If you use MPW, note that these templates are equivalent to the resource type declarations contained in the {RIncludes} directory—refer also to the DeRez command in the *MPW Reference,* and the appropriate chapters of *Inside Macintosh.*)

These are the types you may choose from for your editable data fields:

DBYT, DWRD, DLNG	Decimal byte, decimal word, decimal long word
HBYT, HWRD, HLNG	Hex byte, hex word, hex long word
AWRD, ALNG	Word align, long align
FBYT, FWRD, FLNG	Byte fill, word fill, long fill (with 0)
HEXD	Hex dump of remaining bytes in resource (This can only be the last type in a resource.)
PSTR	Pascal string (length byte followed by the characters)
LSTR	Long string (length long followed by the characters)
WSTR	Same as LSTR, but a word rather than a long word
ESTR, OSTR	Pascal string padded to even or odd length (needed for DITL resources)
CSTR	C string (characters followed by a null)
ECST, OCST	Even-padded C string, or odd-padded C string (padded with nulls)
BOOL	Boolean (two bytes)
BBIT	Binary bit (There must be 8 or an even multiple of 8 of these; if fewer than 8 bits are defined, you must include placeholder bits.)
TNAM	Type name (four characters, like OSType and ResType)
CHAR	A single character
RECT	An 8-byte rectangle
H*nnn*	A 3-digit hex number; displays *nnn* bytes in hex format
C*nnn*	A C string that is *nnn* hex bytes long (The last byte is always a 0, so the string itself occupies the first *nnn*-1 bytes.)

P0*nn*   A Pascal string that is *nn* hex bytes long (The length byte is not included in *nn*, so the string occupies the entire specified length.)

◆ *Note:* Scrolling can become extremely slow if a template contains many BBIT or BOOL items.

ResEdit does the appropriate type checking for you when you put the editing dialog window away.

The template mechanism is flexible enough to describe a repeating sequence of items within a resource, as in `STR#`, `DITL`, and `MENU` resources. You can also have repeating sequences within repeating sequences, as in `BNDL` resources. To terminate a repeating sequence, put the appropriate code in the template as follows:

LSTZ

LSTE   *List Zero–List End.* Terminated by a 0 byte (as in `MENU` resources).

ZCNT

LSTC

LSTE   *Zero Count/List Count–List End.* Terminated by a zero-based word count that starts the sequence (as in `DITL` resources).

OCNT

LSTC

LSTE   *One Count/List Count–List End.* Terminated by a one-based word count that starts the sequence (as in `STR#` resources).

LSTB

LSTE   *List Begin–List End.* Ends at the end of the resource. (As in `acur` and `APPL` resources.)

The LSTB (list-begin) code begins the repeating sequence of items, and the LSTE code is the end. Labels for these codes are usually set to the string "*****". Both of these codes are required. It is generally advisable to keep the beginning and ending labels identical to each other and to have them be no more than five characters long.

Your template does not have to be inside ResEdit; it can be in any open file. (The preferred location is the ResEdit Preferences file in your System Folder.) Note that if more than one currently open file contains a template for your resource type, the one in the most recently opened file is used when you edit resources of your type. To create a template, follow these steps:

1. Open the file into which you want to put your template.
2. Open the 'TMPL' type window. (If no resources of type 'TMPL' exist in the file, choosing Create New Resource from the Resource Menu in the File window opens both the picker and the editor, eliminating step 3.)
3. Choose Create New Resource from the Resource menu.
4. Select the (1)*****) list separator by clicking it.
5. Choose Insert New Field(s) from the Resource menu. You may now begin entering the label, type pairs that define the template. Before closing the template editing window, choose Get Info from the Resource menu and set the name of the template to the four-character name of your resource type.
6. Close the file window and save changes.

The next time you try to edit or create a resource of the new type, you'll get the dialog box in the format you have specified.

Chapter 6 **ResEdit Tips**

As with any other utility, ResEdit takes some getting used to. This chapter presents a few handy tips and a few "hints and kinks" to help you become more comfortable with the capabilities of the program.

Hints and kinks

Some of the examples and suggestions given here are oversimplified to help new users of ResEdit and users who may not be fully familiar with the user interface of the Macintosh computer.

- At the risk of being slightly repetitive, and because these things can be important, it is suggested once again that you edit resources in a copy of your target file, rather than in the original.
- If you choose Get Info for ResEdit (from the Finder), you will find that Application Memory Size is set to 500K. If you are editing large resources 500K is not sufficient, and you should give ResEdit more memory.
- The following sequence of steps can be used to copy a 'PICT' resource from most drawing or painting programs into another file:
  1. Open the file that contains the graphic you want to turn into a 'PICT' resource.
  2. Select and copy the part of the graphic you want.
  3. Start ResEdit and open the file you want to store the 'PICT' resource in.
  4. Open the 'PICT' picker for that file (if the file already has 'PICT' resources in it) by double-clicking the 'PICT' type or by clicking the 'PICT' type and choosing Open 'PICT' Picker from the Resource menu. If the file does not already contain the 'PICT' resource type, create one, which opens the picker and the editor. Close the editor and delete the new resource to get an empty (but open) picker.
  5. Choose Paste from the Edit menu or use the Command-V key combination.

If you paste with the file window open instead of the 'PICT' picker window, you will get both the 'PICT' and the application's private resource type (for example, 'MDPL' if your 'PICT' is from MacDraw).

- To add a picture to a 'DLOG' resource:
  1. Get a picture. Add it to the 'PICT' resources in your file. (See the previous tip.)
  2. Choose the Get Resource Info command from the Resource menu.
  3. Choose Copy from the Edit menu to put the ID number of the new 'PICT' in the scrap.

(Instead of steps 2, 3, and 7 here, you can read the ID number from the screen when you copy the 'PICT' resource, and type it into the 'DITL' item yourself. ResEdit 2.1 displays the ID number of each 'PICT' resource.)

  4. Go to the 'DITL' resource that belongs to the 'DLOG' resource you are adding the picture to.
  5. Drag a 'PICT' from the palette.

6. Choose Open as Dialog Item from the Resource menu or press the Return key. This invokes the Dialog Item editor.
7. Paste the ID number from the scrap.
8. Close the Dialog Item editor.
9. Choose Use Item's Rectangle from the DITL menu.
10. Position the picture by dragging it.

- When you make your own template resources, you may want them to display your own icon instead of the question mark that ResEdit ordinarily displays. Here's how you do it:
    1. Get or make an icon, of resource type `ICON` for black and white or of resource type `icl4` if you want it to display in color.
    2. Put it into the ResEdit Preferences file and give it the same name as your `TMPL` resource.

- If you are using any of the bit editors and you make a selection with the marquee and then cut or copy it, you can paste it into either a file window or the `PICT` picker as a `PICT` resource.

- There are keyboard equivalents for many operations you would ordinarily perform with the mouse. Try selecting a file in the File Open dialog box by typing the first letter or two, then opening it with the Return key; you can do the same with resource types, and then with individual resources. (With individual resources, you can type the ID number or the name.) The arrow keys also work—for example, in a file list, you can go down the list with the down-arrow key.

- There is a hidden Change Color command in the bit editors. If you hold down the Command key and pick a new color, all pixels of the current foreground (or background) color are changed to the new color.

- In general, it is a good idea to use the same ID for an `ALRT` or `DLOG` resource and its associated `DITL` resource, though this practice is not required.

- Other shortcuts and handy items:
    - In a resource picker: use Option–double-click for the Open Using Hex command.
    - In a resource picker: use Option–Command–double-click for the Open Using Template command.
    - In the resource picker, Option–Command–Shift–double-click (or Shift–Open Using Template) displays the template-type dialog box without the list of templates. (You can enter the template type you want.) If you are operating from a floppy disk, this can be a fast method.
    - Option-Cut and Option-Copy append the cut or copied item to the scrap. At the individual item editor level, holding down the Option key does not change the action of the Cut or Copy command.
    - In the `DITL` editor: use Option–Command–double-click on any resource item to open it using its normal editor rather than the `DITL` item editor.

- Command-click in a picker for disjoint selection.
- Shift-click in a picker to extend a selection. (In a pictorial display such as the one for 'ICON' resources, the selection will extend as a rectangle.)
- Using Shift–Create New Resource to create a new resource type gives you the "new type" dialog box without the list of resources. You must, of course, enter the resource type you want rather than selecting it from the list. If you are operating from a floppy disk, this can be a fast method.
- Option-Create New Resource normally creates a new resource and opens it using the hexadecimal editor. If you are creating a 'ppat' or 'ppt#' resource, however, it creates a new relative pattern.

■ If you hold down the Command, Option, and Shift keys while choosing About ResEdit from the Apple menu, you can toggle a special stress-testing mode ("Pig mode"). In this mode, ResEdit performs a compact-memory operation and a purge-memory operation each time it receives an event from the queue, excepting null events. This feature was designed as an aid to debugging ResEdit itself, and is clearly something most people will never have any use for. It is suggested that you avoid invoking this mode unless you are writing an editor and feel a need to stress-test it.

■ Because 'DITL' and 'ALRT' resources are ordinarily displayed where you put them in the window, there is some chance that they may be mispositioned. That is, if you don't have your code display these resources exactly where you want them, they could show up where you *don't* want them. To be sure that a dialog box shows up where you want it, mark it as invisible and reposition it exactly in your code. Have your code mark it visible right after displaying it. (This avoids various embarrassments.)

■ If you have Color QuickDraw, but you want to be able to open the 'ICN#' editor by double-clicking a resource of type 'ICN#' (rather than opening the Finder icon family editor), you can make a resource of type 'RMAP' in the ResEdit Preferences file. This resource should look like the one shown in Figure 6-1. Notice that the name of the 'RMAP' resource is the name of the resource you will be opening, and the MapTo field contains the name of the editor you want to invoke. Set the name of the 'RMAP' resource as usual, with the Get Resource Info command from the Resource menu. If you set Editor Only? to 1, the 'RMAP' is used for the editor but not for the template, if one exists.

- **Figure 6-1**   `'RMAP'` resource

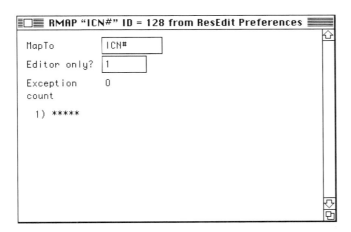

- If you hold down the Option and Command keys and choose About ResEdit from the Apple menu, you get a list of credits that tells you who has worked on the program.

- Although under ordinary conditions the menu ID number and the `'MENU'` resource ID are kept identical to one another, there is one situation in which you may want to make them different. If you are using an ordinary debugger to disassemble and walk through the main event loop of your program, it is convenient to have the Menu Manager return numbers like 1, 2, 3, 4, and 5 for the menus in your program. You would therefore set the menu ID fields of your menus to consecutive integers. Then you might create a `'MBAR'` resource with ID 128 and list the `'MENU'` resource IDs of your menus in it. You need only call `GetNewMBar (128)` in your program to install all of the menus. When you are debugging, a call to `MenuSelect` (for example) returns a value of $00030004 if the fourth item in the third menu has been chosen. This is rather more convenient than seeing $00820004 and having to translate $82 to 130 decimal, and then remembering that 130 was your third menu. If you use a high-level debugger, this approach is unnecessary.

The `'LAYO'` resource

One of the resources inside the Finder is of particular interest, because in system software release 6 it controls a number of defaults, most of which are part of the layout of your desktop. It is the `'LAYO'` resource. To open the Finder with ResEdit, you must be running under the Finder itself (rather than under MultiFinder), or you must edit a copy of the Finder. It is, of course, suggested that you edit a copy. If MultiFinder is running and you try to open the currently active Finder, you get an error message telling you that the Finder is already open from another application.

If you are in a risk-taking mood (or if you have done this a few hundred times already and have become inured to it), boot without MultiFinder, open the Finder, and choose the `'LAYO'` resource type. There is only one `'LAYO'` resource, ID number 128. Open it.

The first part of the template is shown in Figure 6-2.

- **Figure 6-2** `'LAYO'` template, view 1

```
LAYO ID = 128 from Finder
Font ID          3
Font Size        9
Screen Hdr      20
Hgt
Top line       -21
break
Bottom line     17
break
Printing hdr    42
hgt
Printing        32
footer hgt
```

The first two items control the display font—that is, the font that prints out under the icons on your desktop. The default is 9-point Geneva, as shown. If you dislike sans-serif fonts, you can easily change the first two items to 2 and 9, for New York at 9 points, or to 20 and 10 (or even 12), for Times at 10 or 12 points; the 9-point version of Times is very small.

The line of numbers labeled Window Rect in Figure 6-3 allows you to specify the default folder (and disk) window size and location.

■ **Figure 6-3** 'LAYO' template, view 2

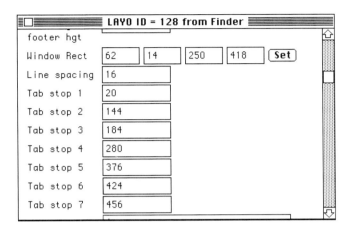

If you like, you can specify these defaults by clicking the Set button and then drawing a rectangle on the screen. Please note that if MultiFinder is running when you edit the 'LAYO' resource in a copy of the Finder, and you try to start your rectangle in an area of the screen that has something other than a ResEdit window in it, you will find yourself summarily ejected from ResEdit into whatever you have clicked. The cure is straightforward: Move a ResEdit window to the area where you want to start drawing your rectangle before you click the Set button, or use the number fields instead of the Set button. You can also explicitly set the locations of the seven tab stops the Finder uses for displaying information about files when you view them by name, date, size, or kind.

A bit further down the template are the numbers that control the placement of the icons themselves, as shown in Figure 6-4.

■ **Figure 6-4** 'LAYO' template, view 3

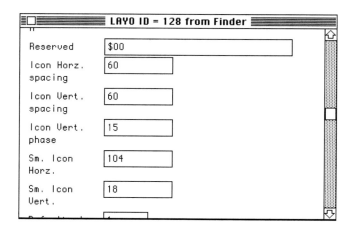

Some people dislike having icons with long names overlapping and obscuring the names of other icons. One solution to this problem is to change the value of "Icon Vert. phase". Figure 6-4 shows some modified numbers, rather than the defaults supplied with the system release.

▲ **Warning**   Do not set "Icon Vert. phase" to exactly half the value of "Icon Vert. spacing" unless you like system crashes. ▲

Figure 6-5 shows some unused bits and three commands, the first of which ("Use zoom Rects") is on by default. If you set it to FALSE, the Finder will open and close windows slightly faster, because it won't use its "zoom" visual effect.

■ **Figure 6-5** 'LAYO' template, view 4

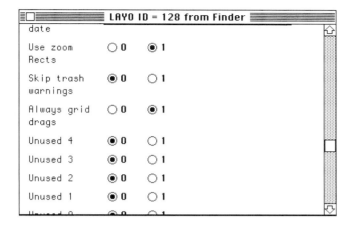

"Skip trash warnings" prevents the system from asking whether you really want to throw away applications or System files. Because you can avoid the warning by holding down the Option key when you throw things into the Trash, this seems a bit extreme. Moreover, it can be quite dangerous, depending on what you tend to throw out and how attentive you are about it.

If you don't like having to clean up your windows, try turning on "Always grid drags". This option makes the icons stick in place at the grid spacing specified in the part of the template shown in Figure 6-4. Some people prefer to be able to put them anywhere and therefore eschew this option.

The Watch Thresh setting (not visible in any of the figures) allows you to adjust how long the Finder will wait during lengthy operations such as file copying before it displays a wristwatch icon with animated hands. The time is expressed in 60ths of a second. If you make it too short, the cursor will jitter and change shape too often. Some older Finders do not make use of this option.

Figure 6-6 shows a few more unused bits and the end of the template.

■ **Figure 6-6** `'LAYO'` template, view 5

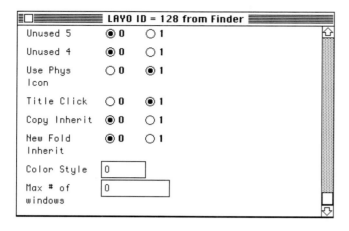

Use Phys Icon is handy if you have a Macintosh II or Macintosh SE with two floppy disk drives. If this option is on, the icon you get when you insert a floppy disk into your machine indicates which drive the floppy disk is in. The disk location is certainly easy enough to recall just after you put the disk in, but you may forget it later. Knowing which drive a floppy disk is in may not be a major issue, but is certainly a pleasant convenience. This option also includes distinctive icons for an external hard disk and a CD-ROM drive.

Title Click lets you double-click the title bar of a folder's window to bring the parent folder's window to the front (or to open it if it is not already open). This feature can be quite handy.

When you create folders on an AppleShare® server, New Fold Inherit causes them to get their privileges from the parent folder, and when you duplicate existing folders on an AppleTalk® server, Copy Inherit causes the copies to inherit their privileges from the originals.

The "Max # of windows" field allows you to set the maximum number of windows the Finder can have open at any one time. Increasing this number causes the Finder to need more memory. Under MultiFinder, you may have to increase the memory allocation for the Finder if you make this number much larger than the default.

Some of the items in the `'LAYO'` template have not been discussed here. Of these, some are not yet in use, and are so marked. Others are either arcane or self-evident.

'KCHR' questions and answers

- How do I change the character generated by Shift-e?

Shift-e normally generates a capital E character. To make this key combination generate a different character, simply hold down the Shift key and use the mouse to drag a character from the character chart to the e key on the keyboard.

You will notice that when you press the Shift key, the table that is highlighted in the table list changes. (For most key layouts, the highlight switches from Table 0 to Table 1.) This change shows you that any character changes you make will be made in the highlighted table. When you make Shift-e generate a different character, you are changing every modifier key combination that uses the highlighted table. For example, if Option-Shift used the same table as Shift, you would also have changed the character generated by Option-Shift-e.

- How do I change the behavior of a modifier key combination?

For example, suppose you wanted Option-Shift-a to generate a different character from that generated by Option-Command-Shift-a. If you hold down the Option and Shift keys and then press and release the Command key, you will notice that (for most key layouts) the highlighted table does not change. If you want these two modifier key combinations to be different, you need to create a new table for one of them. To do this, you can use either the New Table command or the Duplicate Table command from the KCHR menu. If you want to create only a few differences, you should use the Duplicate Table command. In our example, we want only Option-Command-Shift-a to be different, so we would do the following:

1. Press and hold down the Option, Command, and Shift keys.
2. Choose Duplicate Table from the KCHR menu.
3. Select the new table that was added to the end of the list (while still holding down the modifier keys).
4. Choose OK in the alert box that appears.
5. Drag the character from the character chart to the key that you want to change (while still holding down all of the modifier keys).

- How do I remove a table that is no longer being used?

If you have reassigned a modifier key combination so that a table is no longer used, you can remove the table by choosing "Remove unused tables" from the KCHR menu. If there are unused or duplicate tables present when you close the editor, you will be asked whether they should be removed.

- How do I create a dead key?

You can create a dead key (such as Option-e in most key layouts) by choosing "Convert to dead key" from the KCHR menu while holding down the key. For example, follow these steps to make Option-k into a dead key:

1. Press and hold down the Option and k keys.
2. Choose "Convert to dead key" from the KCHR menu.
3. Release the keys.
4. Once again, press Option and k to activate the dead-key editor.

- How do I remove a dead key?

Follow these steps:

1. Select the dead key to display the dead-key editor.
2. Choose "Remove dead key" from the KCHR menu.

- How do I create a new completion/substitution pair in the dead-key editor?

When the dead-key editor is active, you can drag characters from the character chart to the completion/substitution pair list. The character on the left in the list is the completion character, and the character on the right is the substitution character. For example, Option-E followed by Shift-E produces the É character.

- How do I delete a completion/substitution pair in the dead-key editor?

To delete a completion/substitution pair, drag either character from that pair in the completion/substitution pair list to the Trash in the lower-right corner of the window.

Chapter 7 The Programmatic Interface

You may want to create and edit your own types of resources. You can write pickers and editors as extensions to ResEdit in Pascal or C, and put them in the ResEdit Preferences file in your System Folder. This chapter describes this process and discusses necessary and optional functions and procedures.

Pickers and editors

Pickers and editors are separate from ResEdit's main code and therefore may be supplied by user-written software.

The *picker* is given the resource type information and should display all resources of that type in the current resource file, using a suitable display format. If the picker is given an Open call and there is a suitable editor, it should launch that editor. You need not supply your own picker; if a custom picker is not available, the standard picker is used to show a list of resources with their names and IDs.

The *editor* is the code that displays and lets you edit a particular resource. The editor is given a handle to the resource object and should open an edit window for you.

Code-containing resources in the ResEdit release

ResEdit includes three different types of resources that contain code. Much of the code is in the normal `CODE` resources. The editors and pickers are found in the `RSSC` resources, and the LDEF (or list definition) procedures are found in the `LDEF` resources. The resource names of the pickers and editors are very important. The resource name of the `RSSC` resource for a picker should be the resource type that the picker will pick. The resource name for an editor should be the resource type that the editor will edit, with a commercial "at" sign (@) in front of it. **Subeditors** (described in the section "Routines used to start pickers and editors" later in this chapter) should have a dollar sign ($) in front of the resource type name. For example, the `DITL` picker can be found in an `RSSC` resource with the name DITL. The `DITL` editor can be found in an `RSSC` resource with the name @DITL, and the `DITL` subeditor in an `RSSC` resource with the name $DITL.

Samples

A sample resource editor, picker, and LDEF are included with ResEdit. The samples are provided in both C and Pascal and use the MPW 3.2 environment, the MPW C or Pascal Compiler, and the MPW Assembler. The appropriate build files and makefiles are also provided.

Sample editor

A sample ResEdit editor is provided in the file XXXX.Edit. In this sample, *XXXX* represents your resource type. The sample editor will simply display a window and invert its contents. Since the details of editing your resource are known only to you, it is up to you to fill in the code necessary to make this sample into a real editor.

The sample editor is initialized by means of the `EditBirth` procedure when a resource of type XXXX must be edited. `EditBirth` is passed two handles: a handle to the resource to be edited (the same handle that would be received by using a `GetResource` call) and a handle back to the picker that launched the editor.

The editor then creates a window and sets up any data structures needed to operate. Because it may be loaded in and out of memory during any given session and because it doesn't have access to global variables, it creates a handle to a data structure to hold all data that needs to be preserved between calls. Note that the handle to the edit data structure is stored in the window's `refCon` parameter. ResEdit uses this data structure to identify which editor or picker is to receive a given event.

ResEdit determines which editor should receive which events, so you need to worry only about events that affect your editor. During an update event, the `BeginUpdate` and `EndUpdate` calls are done by ResEdit, not by the extension program.

Sample picker

A sample ResEdit picker is provided in the file ICON.Pick. The sample picker is an `'ICON'` picker. The `'ICON'` LDEF (in the file ICON.LDEF) is included with this example so that you can see the interaction between a picker and its LDEF. ResEdit normally uses a `'PICK'` resource for the `'ICON'` picker. If you want to try the example picker you will have to delete the `'PICK'` resource named "ICON" from ResEdit.

Sample LDEF

A sample ResEdit LDEF is provided in the file ICON.LDEF. An LDEF is a list definition procedure used to customize the way the List Manager draws and highlights cells. For more information, see *Inside Macintosh*, Volume IV, Chapter 30, and *Technical Introduction to the Macintosh Family*, Chapter 3. In ResEdit, LDEFs are used to customize the look of the picker windows. LDEFs are generally very simple procedures that draw or highlight a single cell of a list. The sample LDEF is the `'ICON'` LDEF from ResEdit. This LDEF is used to display a file's icons.

Building the examples

You can build the examples by using the build scripts provided in the folder appropriate to the language that you are using. The build scripts assume that ResEdit and the Examples folder will be found in the directory {boot}ResEdit:. If these files are located elsewhere, the build script files should be modified accordingly.

If ResEdit is successfully located, the makefile instructions will install the editor, picker, and LDEFs directly into ResEdit. When you experiment with changing any of these files, you may want to do your build into a duplicate copy of ResEdit rather than your original. If anything goes wrong, you can easily make a fresh duplicate of ResEdit to continue your experiments.

Using ResEd

The program you write must be a Pascal unit or C header file and library. Its interface with ResEdit is established by the MPW unit ResEd, contained in the file ResEd.p or ResEd.h. If your unit is written in Pascal, it must begin with a USES declaration for this unit.

The assembly-language code that "opens up" ResEdit and activates your program is contained in the file RSSC.a. It must be linked with your Pascal or C module. When you open a resource of your type, ResEdit will call this code.

If your build script does not automatically install your editor or picker, place it in ResEdit's file by using ResEdit itself, with the type 'RSSC' and a unique ID number. Please use an ID number between 2500 and 3000 to avoid future conflicts. Use a range of ten numbers, starting with the number that is ten times your editor's ID number for other resources, such as 'DLOG' or 'MENU'. For example, if your editor has ID 2560, your 'DLOG' should have ID 25600. Your editor's name in the ResEdit file must be of the form @ABCD, where *ABCD* is the name you have assigned to the new type it edits. Install your picker (also of type 'RSSC') with the name ABCD (without the commercial "at" sign).

Writing a ResEdit extension

Here are two things to remember when writing a ResEdit extension:

- Always know which resource you are requesting and where it will come from. The ResEdit Preferences file is always the current resource file. This avoids inadvertently loading resources from the file being edited. (For example, `GetNewDialog` could load a `'CDEF'` resource from the file being edited instead of from the System file.) Always use ResEdit's versions of the resource manager calls to be sure you get the resource from the correct file.
- Your editor may be called with an empty handle in order to create an entirely new instance of the type you edit.

In all of these procedures, remember to lock any handle that is going to be dereferenced (for example, in a Pascal `with` statement). For example, in Pascal, the first instructions in the `DoEvent` procedure should be

```
BubbleUp(Handle(object));
HLock(Handle(object));
```

It is important to call the `BubbleUp` procedure to avoid heap fragmentation. Remember to unlock the object at the end of the procedure!

If any of these procedures will need access to the current port, especially `EditBirth`, `DoEvent`, and `DoMenu`, call

```
SetPort (object^^.wind)
```

if you are writing in Pascal, or

```
SetPort ((*object)->wind)
```

if you are writing in C.

ResEdit Menus

ResEdit 2.1 guarantees the following conditions when an activate event is received:

File menu	All items are enabled.
Edit menu	All text is set to default strings except Select All and Select Changed. If a picker window is being activated, all items are enabled. If an editor or floating window is being activated, all but duplicate, select all and select changed are enabled.

Resource menu   All text is set to default strings except Get Resource Info. If a picker window is being activated, all items are enabled. If an editor or floating window is being activated, only Revert and GetInfo are enabled.

Pickers

It's easy to create a new picker with ResEdit 2.1. All you need is a `PICK` resource and an `LDEF` to draw and highlight the cells. You can use the `PICK` template to create a `PICK` resource and create a new `LDEF` using the example code. The `PICK` resource contains the same fields that you would normally initialize in the `PickBirth` procedure before you call `DoPickBirth`. You should put the same values into the resource that you would store into the `PickRec` data structure.

ResEdit 2.0 changes

Here's what you have to do to upgrade an editor to ResEdit 2.0:

- Change the name field of your parent record from `STR64` to `STR255`.
- Add `AbleMenu` for the Resource menu on activate:
    ```
    AbleMenu (rsrcMenu, rsrcEditor);
    ```
- Change `AbleMenu` for the File menu to
    ```
    AbleMenu (fileMenu, fileAll);
    ```
- Add `PrintItem` to the `DoMenu` procedure:
    ```
    printItem:
        PrintWindow (NIL);
    ```
- In `DoMenu`, change `RevertItem` to `rsrcRevertItem` and `GetInfoItem` to `rsrcGetInfoItem`. Move them from the File menu to the Resource menu.
- Add the `IsThisYours` function and be sure to make it public. See the example code for details.
- `EditorWindSetup` now requires a `windowKind` parameter and a `dlogID` parameter; `windowKind` should be the resource ID of the editor or picker (returned by `ResEdID`), and `dlogID` should be `noDialog` or the resource ID of a dialog box to be used for the window.
- `WindOrigin` now takes a `ParentHandle` parameter and requires that the `windowKind` field of the argument window be set to the resource ID of the editor.

ResEd changes for the 2.0 release

Please note these changes:

- `PickRec` was changed to remove some unused fields and add other fields for the View menu.
- `ParentRec` was changed to include an STR255 instead of STR64.
- Menu and string constants were changed.
- Several procedures have interface changes; these are the new interfaces:

```
FUNCTION   EditorWindSetup (dlogID: INTEGER; colorkind: ColorType; width,
        height: INTEGER; VAR windowTitle, windowName: STR255; addFrom:
        BOOLEAN; windowKind: INTEGER; father: ParentHandle): WindowPtr;

PROCEDURE WindOrigin (w: WindowPtr; dad: ParentHandle);

PROCEDURE PickMenu (tossOnClose: BOOLEAN; menu, item: INTEGER; pick:
        PickHandle);
```

ResEdit 2.1 changes

Here's the information you need to update an editor from ResEdit 2.0 to ResEdit 2.1:

- The `ParentRec` data structure has changed, as have all other derived structures. Five new fields have been added. You should initialize them as follows:

```
windowType := editorWindow;
theResType := 'PAT ';   { or whatever }
theResFile := HomeResFile (thing);   { thing is the res handle
                                       passed to EditBirth }
codeResID := ResEdID;
theResToEdit := thing;
```

- You no longer have to start the name saved in `ParentRec` with an `editorNameChr`. The `windowType` field of `ParentRec` now indicates that an editor owns the window.
- The boolean color parameter of `EditorWindSetup` has changed to a tri-state `colorKind` parameter. If you don't need a color window, change FALSE to noColor.
- You may no longer need to set and reset the menus when you receive activate and deactivate events. See the section on ResEdit menus in this chapter.
- Several procedure names were changed:

```
NewRes => RENewUniqueRes
AddNewRes => REAddNewRes
```

```
BeautifulUnique1ID => REBeautifulUnique1ID
ResEditGet1Resource => REGet1ResourceSpecial
RemoveResource => RERemoveAnyResource
Get1Res => REGet1Resource
Get1Index => REGet1IndResource
```

- Several new procedures have been added:
    - Window utilities

        `FloatingWindowSetup`

    - Extended resource manager

        `REAddResource`

        `RECount1Resources`

        `RECount1Types`

        `REGet1IndType`

        `REGet1NamedResource`

    - Routines used to feed events and menus to the appropriate picker or editor

        `CallDoEvent`

        `PassEvent`

    - Miscellaneous utilities

        `ChooseIcon`

        `HandleCheck`

        `StandardFilter`

    - Pop-up menus

        `DoPopup`

        `DrawPopup`

    - Internal routines

        `CompressedResource`

        `DoKeyScan`

        `GetResEditScrapFile`

- The following procedures have been removed:

`CurrentRes` (use `CurResFile` instead)

`Get1MapEntry`

`MyCalcMask`

`ScrapPaste`

- The following changes have been made for pickers:
  - `PickRec` now includes three new fields:
    - `minWindowWidth`
    - `minWindowHeight`
    - `optionCreateStr`
  - The following fields have been removed from `PickRec`:
    - `rNum` (replaced by `theResFile`)
    - `drawProc` (was unused)
    - `scroll` (was unused)
    - `pickID` (replaced by `codeResID`)
  - In most cases, specific pickers are no longer needed, though you still need an LDEF. A new resource type, `'PICK'`, specifies everything ResEdit needs to know about a picker (in 20 bytes!). ResEdit 2.1 includes a template for editing `'PICK'` resources.

Required routines

Each picker and editor must contain a set of required procedures. Some of these procedures are appropriate only for editors, and others are appropriate only for pickers, but all of them must appear in all editors and pickers.

`PROCEDURE EditBirth (theResource: Handle; dad: ParentHandle);`

This procedure should initialize the editor data structure and create an editor window for the given resource type. In a picker, this procedure will do nothing and should be defined as

```
PROCEDURE EditBirth (theResource: Handle; dad: ParentHandle);
BEGIN
END;
```

`PROCEDURE PickBirth (theType: ResType; dad: ParentHandle);`

This procedure should initialize the picker data structure and create a picker window for the given type. `PickBirth` is very similar to `EditBirth` except that it takes a resource type as a parameter instead of a resource handle. The `DoPickBirth` procedure can usually be used to take care of most initialization for a picker. In an editor, this procedure will do nothing and should be defined as

```
PROCEDURE PickBirth (theType: ResType; dad: ParentHandle);
BEGIN
END;
```

```
PROCEDURE DoEvent(VAR evt: EventRecord; object: ParentHandle);
```

`DoEvent` handles all events for the picker or editor. The object parameter can be locally defined as whatever type is appropriate (such as a `PickHandle`) instead of the generic `ParentHandle`.

Editors will normally handle all of the events (except those described in the next paragraph) themselves, whereas pickers should simply call `PickEvent`.

Many events are handled by the main part of the ResEdit code before the `DoEvent` procedure is called. For mouse-down events, ResEdit handles the following events: pulling down menus, dragging windows, switching between windows, and converting double-clicks to open commands. Update events call `BeginUpdate` and `EndUpdate` around the call to `DoEvent`. For key-down events, the `DoMenu` procedure is called if the Command key was down (unless the key was Return, Enter, or an arrow key); `DoEvent` is called otherwise. MultiFinder suspend and resume events are converted into the appropriate activate or deactivate events.

```
PROCEDURE DoInfoUpdate(oldID, newID: INTEGER; object: ParentHandle);
```

This procedure is called when information about a resource—for example, its ID number—is changed in a Get Info window. (See the `ShowInfo` procedure, discussed later in this chapter in the section "Miscellaneous Utilities.") For editors, the `DoInfoUpdate` procedure should recalculate the window title and the name stored in the `ParentHandle` and pass the update on to its father by using the `CallInfoUpdate` procedure as follows:

```
CallInfoUpdate(oldID, newID, LONGINT(object^^.father),
object^^.father^^.wind^.windowKind);
```

Pickers should simply call

```
PickInfoUp (oldID, newID, object);
```

```
PROCEDURE DoMenu(menu, item: INTEGER; object: ParentHandle);
```

`DoMenu` handles all menu events for the picker or editor. The object parameter can be locally defined as whatever type is appropriate (such as a `PickHandle`) instead of the generic `ParentHandle`.

The main part of the ResEdit code takes care of several of the menu-handling details. All selections from the Apple menu are handled so that the editors and pickers do not need to know anything about desk accessories. All commands in the File menu are also handled for you. The Quit command displays the Save Changes dialog box and may pass a Close command to all editors and pickers. If your editor needs to do some cleaning up before the Quit command completes, it should do so when it receives a Close or deactivate command. If "no" is chosen in the Save File dialog box, the frontmost window receives a deactivate event. No events are passed to any other window. When your editor receives a Close command, it can call `CloseNoSave` to see whether edit checking should be performed. If the current file is being closed but the changes are not being saved, `CloseNoSave` will return TRUE, and edit checking should not be performed.

Pickers can simply call

```
PickMenu (menu, item, object);
```

The ResEd interface

The ResEd unit contains data structures, procedures, and functions that you can access from your extension program. They are described in the remainder of this chapter.

Data structures

The ResEd unit declares the data structures described in this section, which provide communication between extension programs and ResEdit. Each editor or picker has its own object handle. The data structure has to start with a handle to its parent's object, followed by a unique name. The next field should be the window of the object that may be used by the child to get back to the father through the `refCon` in the `windowRec` record. The next field is the "rebuild" field, a flag used to indicate that a window's data (for example, a picker's list) must be recalculated at the next opportunity. Next is a `resWasntLoaded` flag, which should be set by calling `WasItLoaded` in the `EditBirth` procedure. If the value of `resWasntLoaded` is FALSE, the resource being edited should not be released. Next is `WindowType`, which indicates the type of the window. The field `TheResType` is the type of the resource, `TheResFile` is the file reference number of the file containing the resource, `CodeResID` is the ID of the `'RSSC'` resource containing the editor or picker, and `TheResToEdit` is the resource being edited. For editors, the rest of the handle can have any format; pickers have additional data, as described in this chapter. Editors and pickers typically declare additional fields at the end of the predefined fields and can store in these additional fields global data that they need to access from the `DoEvent`, `DoInfoUpdate`, and `DoMenu` procedures.

The name (in the `ParentRecord`) for a picker should be the name of the file. For editors, the name should be the complete name (not the window's title). An example of a complete name is *ALRT ID = -1234 from AFile*. This name is used as a unique identifier for a window. The window's title is created by `GetWindowTitle` or `EditorWindSetup`, described later in this chapter.

◆ *Note:* It is important for editors and pickers to follow these conventions for name and window title. For pickers, it is more important that the window's title be unique, and for editors, that the name be unique. The `AlreadyOpen` procedure uses the window's name and title to determine whether the window is open. Please refer to the description of `AlreadyOpen` later in this chapter in the section "Window Utilities" for complete information about how the name and title are used.

The parent record

Here is the parent record:

```
PossibleWindowTypes =   (typePickerWindow, resourcePickerWindow,
                        folderInfoWindow, fileInfoWindow,
                        resourceInfoWindow, editorWindow,
                        floatingWindow);

ParentPtr = ^ParentRec;
ParentHandle = ^ParentPtr;

ParentRec = RECORD
    father:             ParentHandle;
    name:               str255;
    wind:               WindowPeek;         { Owning window }
    rebuild:            BOOLEAN;            { Flag set when window should
                                              be rebuilt }
    resWasntLoaded:     BOOLEAN;            { TRUE if the resource should
                                              be released when the window
                                              is closed }
    windowType:         PossibleWindowTypes;
    theResType:         ResType;            { Type of the resource }
    theResFile:         INTEGER;            { Home resfile of the res }
    codeResID:          INTEGER;            { Resource ID of the RSSC
                                              resource containing the
                                              picker or editor }
    theResToEdit:       Handle;
END;
```

The picker record

The record for pickers is slightly different from the standard parent record. The first few fields are the same as those in the parent record, but several extra fields have been added.

```
PickPtr = ^PickRec;
PickHandle = ^PickPtr;
ViewTypes = (viewById, viewByName, viewBySize,
             viewByOrder, viewBySpecial);
PickRec = RECORD
    father:           ParentHandle;        { Back ptr to dad }
    fName:            STR255;
    wind:             WindowPtr;           { Picker window }
    rebuild:          BOOLEAN;
    spare1:           BOOLEAN;             { Not used here}
    windowType:       PossibleWindowTypes;
    theResType:       ResType;             { Type of the resource }
    theResFile:       INTEGER;             { Home resfile of the res }
    codeResID:        INTEGER;             { Resource ID of the RSSC
                                             resource containing the
                                             picker or editor }

    spare:            Handle;              { Not used here}
    rType:            ResType;             { Type for picker. }
    rSize:            LONGINT;             { Size of an empty resource }
    minWindowWidth:   INTEGER;             { Used when window is grown }
    minWindowHeight:  INTEGER;
    instances:        ListHandle;          { List of instances }
    nInsts:           INTEGER;             { Number of instances }
    viewBy:           ViewTypes;           { Current view type }
    showAttributes:   BOOLEAN;             { Show attrs in window?}
    ldefType:         ResType;             { Which LDEF to use }
    theViewMenu:      MenuHandle;          { The picker view menu }
    viewMenuMask:     LONGINT;             { Which items are enabled? }
    cellSize:         Cell;                { Cell size for special view }
    optionCreateStr:  STR255;              { Create item menu text when
                                             the option key is pressed }
END;
```

Other routines

The required routines are called by ResEdit itself. Here are others you can use. These are called by the editor or picker.

Window utilities

```
FUNCTION AlreadyOpen (VAR windowTitle, windowName: STR255;
     father: ParentHandle): BOOLEAN;
```

The `AlreadyOpen` routine checks whether the window is already open. If the window is open, `AlreadyOpen` activates it and returns TRUE. The `windowTitle` and `windowName` parameters are as defined in the note immediately below. You don't need to call this function if you are using the `DoPickBirth`, `PickerWindSetup`, or `EditorWindSetup` procedure.

◆ *Note:* You should call `AlreadyOpen` to avoid opening the same resource twice. Correct functioning of `AlreadyOpen` depends on your setting `windowTitle` and `windowName` correctly. For pickers, the window's title must uniquely identify the window. For editors, the name stored in the `parentRec` data structure must uniquely identify the window. The name is used for editors so that the window title can be simple and short. For example, the window title for a dialog item might be `Edit DITL item #3`, whereas its name would be `Edit DITL item #3 • DITL "<resource name>" id = <num> from <filename>`.

```
FUNCTION EditorWindSetup (dlogID: INTEGER; colorKind: ColorType;
     width, height: INTEGER; VAR windowTitle, windowName: STR255;
     addFrom: BOOLEAN; windowKind: INTEGER; father: ParentHandle):
     WindowPtr;
```

The `EditorWindSetup` function should be called by editors from the `EditBirth` procedure to set up their windows. The `windowTitle`, `windowName`, and `addFrom` parameters are passed directly to `GetWindowTitle`. Refer to the description of `GetWindowTitle` for details about these parameters. The `windowName` parameter is returned with the string that should be used for the name in `ParentRecord`. This routine also takes care of constructing the `windowTitle` and `windowName` correctly so that the window can be uniquely identified. Use the `dlogID` parameter if you want your window to be a dialog; for normal windows, pass the constant `noDialog`. If `dlogID` is not set to `noDialog`, the width and height parameters should be set to 0 if you want to use the size stored in the `'DLOG'` resource. The `windowkind` parameter is used to initialize the window. Pass the result of a `ResEdID` call here. The `colorKind` parameter can contain `noColor`, `canColor`, or `requiresColor`. If it's set to `RequiresColor`, the window won't be activated if color is not available.

◆ *Note:* NIL is returned if the window can't be allocated for some reason or if the window is already allocated (that is, an editor is already open). If NIL is returned, the `EditBirth` procedure should be aborted.

```
FUNCTION  FloatingWindowSetup (WINDID: INTEGER;
      fw: FloatingWindowHandle;
      owner: ParentHandle;
      where: Point): WindowPtr;
```

The `FloatingWindowSetup` function allocates a floating palette window (for example, the one used by the `'DITL'` editor). The `WINDID` parameter specifies the resource ID of a `'WIND'` resource that defines the floating window. The `FloatingWindowHandle` parameter is the version of `ParentHandle` used by floating windows. The `owner` parameter specifies the editor window that will control the floating window. The `where` parameter specifies the location of the new floating window. If `where` is 0,0 the floating window will be placed next to the owner window. NIL is returned if the window could not be created.

```
PROCEDURE GetWindowTitle (VAR windowTitle, windowName: STR255;
      addFrom: BOOLEAN; father: ParentHandle);
```

The `GetWindowTitle` procedure constructs the window title and name for an editor. This routine should always be called in the `DoInfoUpdate` procedure, and should be called in the `EditBirth` procedure if `EditorWindSetup` is not called. The value in `windowTitle` should be used for the window's title. The `addFrom` parameter determines whether the name of the file is added to the title. The value in `windowName` should be saved in the name field of the editor's data structure. This name is used later to identify the window uniquely. On input, `windowTitle` should contain only the title or the resource (for example, `'ALRT'`), and `windowName` should contain the resource type (for example, `'ALRT'`). If `EditorWindSetup` is not used, the following code fragment can be used to ensure that the name and title are correct:

```
GetResInfo(myResource, theID, theType, windowTitle);
TypeToString (theType, windowTitle);
SetETitle(myResource, windowTitle);
windowName := windowTitle;
GetWindowtitle (windowTitle, windowName, TRUE, parent);
```

```
FUNCTION  PickerWindSetup(colorKind: ColorType;
    ShowTheWindow: BOOLEAN; width, height: INTEGER;
    VAR windowTitle: STR255; windowKind: INTEGER;
    dad: ParentHandle): WindowPtr;
```

The `PickerWindSetup` function should be called by pickers from the `PickBirth` procedure. It is similar to the `EditorWindSetup` procedure. The `ShowTheWindow` parameter specifies whether the window should be displayed after it is initialized.

```
PROCEDURE SetETitle (h: Handle; VAR title: STR255);
```

The `SetETitle` procedure concatenates the resource ID to the resource name and appends the result to `title`. The `h` parameter is the handle to the resource. You can use this routine when you are constructing a window's name or title.

```
FUNCTION WindAlloc: WindowPtr;
```

The `WindAlloc` function returns a pointer to a window record to be used by your editor or picker. Using this routine instead of allocating your own window pointer can help reduce heap fragmentation. Because windows are pointers and must be nonrelocatable objects in the heap, ResEdit uses this procedure to try to allocate `WindowPtr` pointers as low in the heap as possible. When this procedure is called, it usually returns a `WindowPtr` that it has previously allocated low in the heap.

```
PROCEDURE WindReturn (w: WindowPtr);
```

`WindReturn` returns a window pointer that was allocated by `WindAlloc`. Use this procedure when you terminate your editor or picker and you are finished with its window. The `WindReturn` procedure makes the memory used by the window available to another picker or editor for use as a new window. This helps keep the nonrelocatable window pointers as low in the heap as possible.

Extended resource manager

Because the current resource file is always left set to the ResEdit Preferences file (to avoid loading code resources such as 'LDEF's and 'CDEF's from the wrong file), you should always use the extended resource manager calls to get resources from the file being edited.

```
FUNCTION REAddNewRes (resFile: INTEGER; hNew: Handle;
    t: ResType; idNew: INTEGER; s: str255): BOOLEAN;
```

The REAddNewRes function has similar parameters to, and performs the same actions as, the Macintosh procedure AddResource. If an error is detected, an alert box is displayed and FALSE is returned; TRUE is returned otherwise. The resFile parameter specifies the file to which the resource should be added.

```
PROCEDURE REAddResource(resFile: INTEGER; theResource: Handle;
        theType: ResType;theID: INTEGER;     name: Str255);
```

The REAddResource procedure is similar to the AddResource Toolbox procedure except that it takes resFile as a parameter.

```
FUNCTION REBeautifulUnique1ID (resFile: INTEGER;
    t: ResType): INTEGER;
```

This routine should be used instead of the Toolbox procedure Unique1ID. It returns the first unused resource ID starting with ID 128 in the file specified by resFile.

```
FUNCTION   RECount1Resources(resFile: INTEGER;
        theType: ResType): INTEGER;
```

The RECount1Resources function is similar to the Count1Resources Toolbox procedure except that it takes resFile as a parameter.

```
FUNCTION   RECount1Types (resFile: INTEGER): INTEGER;
```

The RECount1Types function is similar to the Count1Types Toolbox procedure except that it takes resFile as a parameter.

```
FUNCTION REGet1IndResource (resFile: INTEGER;
       theType: ResType; index: INTEGER): Handle;
```

The REGet1IndResource function is similar to the Get1IndResource trap. The only differences are that it takes resFile as a parameter, and that if the resource is not found, it sets ResError to the resNotFound error and returns NIL.

```
PROCEDURE REGet1IndType(resFile: INTEGER;
        VAR theType: ResType;index: INTEGER);
```

The `REGet1IndType` procedure is similar to the `Get1IndType` Toolbox procedure except that it takes `resFile` as a parameter.

```
FUNCTION  REGet1NamedResource(resFile: INTEGER;
        theType: ResType;    name: Str255): Handle;
```

The `REGet1NamedResource` function is similar to the `Get1NamedResource` Toolbox procedure except that it takes `resFile` as a parameter.

```
FUNCTION REGet1Resource (resFile: INTEGER;
      theType: ResType; theID: INTEGER): Handle;
```

The `REGet1Resource` function is similar to the `Get1Resource` trap. The only differences are that it takes `resFile` as a parameter, and that if the resource is not found, it sets `ResError` to the `resNotFound` error and returns NIL.

```
FUNCTION  REGet1ResourceSpecial (resFile: INTEGER;
       theType: ResType; ID: INTEGER; VAR wasLoaded: BOOLEAN;
       VAR error: INTEGER): Handle;
```

The `REGet1ResourceSpecial` function should be used in place of the Toolbox routine `Get1Resource`. It's equivalent to `Get1Resource` except for the fact that it returns a `wasLoaded` variable to indicate whether the resource is already in use. If the return value of `wasLoaded` is TRUE, the caller should *never* free the resource with the `ReleaseResource` procedure.

```
FUNCTION RENewUniqueRes (resFile: INTEGER; s: LONGINT;
       t: ResType;): Handle;
```

Given a size, `s`, `RENewUniqueRes` allocates a new handle, clears it, adds it to the specified resource file as a resource of type `t` with a unique ID, and returns a handle to the new resource. If this function fails, it returns a NIL handle.

```
PROCEDURE RERemoveAnyResource (resFile: INTEGER;
      theRes: Handle);
```

This procedure should always be used in place of the Toolbox call, `RmveResource`. It correctly handles resources that have the protected attribute set, by unprotecting them before removing them. The function of this routine is otherwise the same as that of the `RmveResource` Toolbox procedure.

```
FUNCTION RevertThisResource (theObj: ParentHandle;
    res: Handle): BOOLEAN;
```

The `RevertThisResource` function restores a resource being edited to its state before editing started. The parameter `res` is a handle to the resource. The parameter `theObj` is the `ParentHandle` from the current window. It is needed to determine whether the resource was newly added. The `RevertThisResource` function returns a value of FALSE if the resource was newly added by ResEdit (and, therefore, no longer exists after the reversion), and TRUE otherwise. If the resource has not been changed (its `resChanged` flag is not set), nothing is done.

Routines used by pickers

```
FUNCTION DefaultListCellSize:INTEGER;
```

The `DefaultListCellSize` function returns the height of a list cell with the application font (ascent + descent + leading). This function should be used by pickers that display resources as text strings when setting up their window.

```
FUNCTION  DoPickBirth(colorKind: ColorType;
    buildList: BOOLEAN; which: PICKERTYPE;
    pickerResId: INTEGER; pick: PickHandle): BOOLEAN;
```

The `DoPickBirth` function takes care of just about everything needed to initialize a picker. If the value of `buildList` is TRUE, the list of all of the resources will be created. The `pick` parameter is the handle to a partially initialized `PickHandle`. The fields that should be initialized before this procedure is called are: `father`, `rType`, `viewBy`, `cellSize`, `ldefType`, `minWindowWidth`, and `minWindowHeight`. The example picker shows how these fields should be initialized. The size of the picker's window is calculated automatically from `cellSize`.

```
PROCEDURE DrawLDEF (message: INTEGER; lSelect: BOOLEAN;
    lRect: Rect; theRes: Handle; id: INTEGER;
    title: STR255; maxH, maxV: INTEGER;
    DrawResource: ProcPtr; lh: ListHandle);
```

The `DrawLDEF` procedure is a general-purpose drawing routine for graphic LDEFs such as `'ICON'`, `'cicn'`, and so on. It should be called from an LDEF that is used by a picker. If `title` is an empty string, `id` is converted to a string and used as the title. The `drawProc` is of the form

```
PROCEDURE DrawResource (lRect: Rect; theRes: Handle).
```

Use of this procedure is shown in the example picker LDEF.

```
PROCEDURE GrowMyWindow (minWidth, minHeight: INTEGER;
      windPtr: WindowPtr; lh: ListHandle);
```

Pickers use this procedure to change the size of their windows. The `minWidth` and `minHeight` parameters determine the minimum size of the window; `windPtr` is the window to be resized; `lh` is the list that is in the window.

The `GrowMyWindow` procedure takes care of everything that is necessary to change the size of a picker's window. If necessary, the list is resized and redrawn. Two-dimensional lists (such as those used by the icon picker) are updated to fit as many cells as possible in the window without requiring horizontal scrolling.

```
PROCEDURE PickEvent (VAR evt: EventRecord; pick: PickHandle);
```

The `PickEvent` procedure handles an event contained in `evt` for a standard picker referenced by `pick`. This procedure should be called from your picker's `DoEvent` procedure. It is usually sufficient to call only this routine from `DoEvent`, with no other special processing at all.

```
PROCEDURE PickInfoUp (oldID, newID: INTEGER;
      pick: PickHandle);
```

The `PickInfoUp` procedure handles the update necessary when a resource's ID is changed in the Get Info window. This procedure should be called from your picker's `DoInfoUpdate` procedure. It is usually sufficient to call only this routine from `DoInfoUpdate`, with no other special processing at all.

```
PROCEDURE PickMenu (menu, item: INTEGER; pick: PickHandle);
```

`PickMenu` handles menu commands for a standard picker referenced by `pick`. `PickMenu` should be called from your picker's `DoMenu` procedure. This routine handles all of the standard menu commands. It is usually sufficient to call only this routine from `DoMenu`.

```
FUNCTION  PickStdHeight: INTEGER;
```

This function returns the height in pixels that should be used when creating picker windows. This value is obtained from the Preferences dialog box. A window of the specified height is guaranteed to fit on the screen. Because the picker's size is set by `DoPickBirth`, you should not need to use this procedure.

```
FUNCTION  PickStdWidth: INTEGER;
```

This function returns the width in pixels that should be used when creating picker windows. This value is obtained from the Preferences dialog box. A window of the specified width is guaranteed to fit on the screen. Because the picker's size is set by `DoPickBirth`, you should not need to use this procedure.

Routines used by editors

```
FUNCTION CloseNoSave: BOOLEAN;
```

The `CloseNoSave` function returns a Boolean value that indicates whether data checking should be performed before closing. A return value of TRUE indicates that checking should not be performed. For example, if the user is editing a template and there are errors in the template when the Quit command is chosen, the template editor should not perform edit checking if No was clicked in the Save Changes dialog box.

```
FUNCTION NeedToRevert (myWindow: WindowPtr; theRes: Handle):
    BOOLEAN;
```

The `NeedToRevert` function should be called by all editors before they revert their resource. If the editor's window is frontmost and the resource has been changed, an alert box is displayed asking the user to verify that he or she really wants to revert the resource. If the user does want to revert the resource, the function returns a value of TRUE. Otherwise it returns a value of FALSE. The `myWindow` parameter is a pointer to the editor's window. The `theRes` parameter is the handle of the resource that is to be reverted.

```
PROCEDURE NoDoubleClickHere;
```

Call this procedure in your mouse-down processing code if you don't want ResEdit to convert a double-click at this location to an Open command. This should be used if a double-click makes sense only in part of your window.

```
PROCEDURE SetResChanged (h: Handle);
```

The `SetResChanged` procedure sets the `resChanged` attribute for the specified resource and also sets the `mapChanged` attribute for the resource file that contains the resource. This procedure should be called whenever a resource is changed.

```
FUNCTION  WasItLoaded: BOOLEAN;
```

The `WasItLoaded` function should be called by every editor in the `EditBirth` procedure. The returned value should be saved in the `ParentRec` data structure. When a Close command is received, the resource being edited should be released only if `WasItLoaded` returned FALSE. If the returned value is TRUE, the resource may already be in use by ResEdit or the system and therefore shouldn't be released.

Routines used to start pickers and editors

`PROCEDURE GiveEBirth (resHandle: Handle; pick: PickHandle);`

The `GiveEBirth` procedure starts an editor. This routine is used when a picker wants to start an editor or when an editor wants to start another editor (as when the `'DLOG'` editor starts the `'DITL'` editor). If the user chooses Open Using Template, or if an editor is not found, the `'GNRL'` (template) editor is started. If the user chooses Open Using Hex Editor or if neither an editor nor a template is found, the hexadecimal editor is started. A call to the appropriate editor's `EditBirth` procedure is then generated, as follows:

`EditBirth (resHandle, pick)`

In this call, `resHandle` is the handle of the resource to be edited, and `pick` is the caller's `ParentHandle`.

◆ *Note:* When an editor is starting another editor, it is important to remember that `pick^^.rType` must be set before this routine is called. The editor's `ParentRec` will need to be equivalent to a `PickRec`, at least down to the `rType` field. The `GiveEBirth` procedure looks to the `PickHandle` parameter for information (for example, the resource type) that it needs to start up an editor.

`PROCEDURE GiveSubEBirth (resHandle: Handle; pick: PickHandle);`

The `GiveSubEBirth` procedure starts an editor that edits a part of another type of resource. For example, the `'DITL'` editor uses `GiveSubEBirth` to start the dialog item editor. The `GiveSubEBirth` procedure behaves exactly like `GiveEBirth` except that the name of the resource that it looks for begins with a dollar sign ($) instead of a commercial "at" sign (@). For example, the name of the `'DITL'` editor resource is @DITL and the name of the `'DITL'` subeditor resource is $DITL. This distinction allows an editor to use the standard method for editing multiple occurrences of a subtype within the resource. For example, a dialog item list (`'DITL'`) typically contains several dialog items. Calling `GiveSubEBirth` lets the user open multiple dialog items and treat them in the same way as any other windows.

`PROCEDURE GiveThisEBirth (resHandle: Handle; pick: PickHandle;`
`        openThisType:ResType);`

The `GiveThisEBirth` procedure is similar to `GiveEBirth`, except that it lets the caller specify the type of editor to open. The specified editor is opened even if the user chooses Open Using Template or Open Using Hex Editor. If an editor of the specified type is not found, a template of the specified type is opened. If a template is not found, the hexadecimal editor is opened.

Routines used to feed events and menus to the appropriate picker or editor

```
PROCEDURE CallDoEvent (evt: EventRecord; theWindow:
    WindowPtr);
```

The `CallDoEvent` procedure calls the `DoEvent` procedure of the specified window with the specified event. You normally won't need to use this procedure.

```
PROCEDURE CallInfoUpdate (oldID, newID: INTEGER;
    refcon: LONGINT; id: INTEGER );
```

The `CallInfoUpdate` procedure passes an information update command to the specified window. After updating its own window and data structures, each editor's `DoInfoUpdate` procedure should call this routine to pass the information update along to its parent window. This call is necessary since the parent may be displaying data (such as the ID or name in a picker window) that has been changed. An editor could pass this information along by making the following call:

```
CallInfoUpdate (oldid, newid, longint(father),
father^^.wind^.windowkind);
```

```
PROCEDURE PassEvent (evt: EventRecord; father: ParentHandle);
```

The `PassEvent` procedure sends the specified event to all windows opened by the window owned by the specified `ParentHandle`. You normally won't need to use this procedure.

```
PROCEDURE PassMenu (menu, item: INTEGER; father:
    ParentHandle);
```

The `PassMenu` procedure passes menu commands on to any child pickers or editors that you have started. For example, when your editor receives a Close command, it should make this call to pass that command along to any subeditors or information windows that it has opened:

```
PassMenu (fileMenu, closeItem, myObj)
```

Miscellaneous utilities

```
PROCEDURE Abort;
```

The `Abort` procedure sets the abort flag, which will stop any command that is in progress. The most common use of this command is in stopping the Quit command. For example, if an error is detected in a template when its window is being closed, the template editor calls `Abort` so that processing of the Quit command will stop and the error can be corrected.

`PROCEDURE AbleMenu (menu: INTEGER; enable: LONGINT);`

The `AbleMenu` procedure enables or disables menu items. This procedure differs from the Resource Manager routines `EnableItem` and `DisableItem` in that it acts on the entire menu. The parameter `menu` is a menu ID; `enable` is a mask. Values used for the mask can be found in the ResEd file.

`PROCEDURE BubbleUp (h: Handle);`

The `BubbleUp` procedure sets up the correct heap zone and then calls the Memory Manager routine `MoveHHI`. For information about `MoveHHi`, see *Inside Macintosh,* Volume II, Chapter 1. This routine should always be called, to avoid heap fragmentation, before the Macintosh procedure `HLock` is called for any handle. Remember to unlock any handle that you lock!

`PROCEDURE CenterDialog (theType: ResType; dialog: INTEGER);`

This procedure centers dialogs or alerts on the same screen as the current port, which is assumed to be a window. If the dialog is in color, it is centered on the deepest screen on which any portion of the current port appears. The `ResType` parameter can be "DLOG" or "ALRT"; `dialog` is the resource ID of the dialog or alert. The `'DLOG'` or `'ALRT'` resource is loaded into memory and its `boundsRect` is centered. When you use the dialog or alert box (for example, in `GetNewDialog`), the resource will be found in memory with the correct `boundsRect`.

`FUNCTION CheckError (err, msgID: INTEGER): BOOLEAN;`

The `CheckError` function displays an error alert if the value of `err` is not 0. This routine has built-in alert messages for several errors (such as "disk write-protected", "out of memory", and so on). If the value of `msgId` is negative, a fatal error message is retrieved from the `'STR#'` resource with ID of 128. This resource is preloaded into memory and may be accessible even if a serious error has occurred. If the value of `msgID` is nonnegative, an error message from the `'STR#'` resource with ID of 129 is displayed. If the error is not one that is built in, the string with an ID of `msgID` is displayed in the alert box. TRUE is returned if `err` was 0; FALSE otherwise. When adding a new string for use by `CheckError`, be sure to add it to the end of the existing list in the `'STR#'` resource.

```
FUNCTION  ChooseIcon(EdHandle: ParentHandle;
    VAR IconResID: integer; VAR IconKind: IconType;
    dialogID: integer): BOOLEAN;
```

The `ChooseIcon` function displays the `'ICON'` chooser used by the `'MENU'` and `'BNDL'` editors. The `EdHandle` parameter is the `ParentHandle` of the editor displaying the dialog. Passing `onlyICON` in the `IconKind` parameter forces the IconChooser to not allow reduced `'ICON'`s or `'SICN'`s. Passing `onlyICNPound` in the `IconKind` parameter uses `'ICN#'` resources instead of `'ICON'`s. Passing any other value instructs the IconChooser to support regular `'ICON'`s, reduced `'ICON'`s, and `'SICN'`s (as in the `'MENU'` editor). The icon's resource ID is returned in `IconResID` (this field also specifies the icon to be selected). The `dialogID` field specifies the resource ID of the dialog to be displayed. You should copy the `'MENU'` or `'BNDL'` editor's dialog and make minor changes. Don't remove any of the existing fields. If you don't want some of the fields in your dialog, move them outside of the window bounds.

```
FUNCTION  ColorAvailable (needColorQD: BOOLEAN): BOOLEAN;
```

The `ColorAvailable` function returns TRUE if color QuickDraw is available. If the value of the `needColorQD` parameter is TRUE, an alert is displayed if color QuickDraw is not available.

```
PROCEDURE ConcatStr (VAR str1: STR255; str2: STR255);
```

The `ConcatStr` procedure concatenates `str2` to `str1`, leaving the result in `str1`.

▲ **Warning** This routine does not check for aggregate string lengths in excess of 255 characters. Please be careful! ▲

```
FUNCTION DisplayAlert (which: AlertType; id: INTEGER):
    INTEGER;
```

The `DisplayAlert` function displays an alert box with the given `id`. This routine assures that the alert resource is loaded from ResEdit and that the cursor is reset to an arrow. The `which` parameter determines the kind of alert box that is displayed.

```
AlertType = (displayTheAlert, displayStopAlert, displayNoteAlert,
displayCautionAlert);
```

```
FUNCTION  DisplaySTRAlert(which: AlertType; STRName: STR255;
    STRIndex: INTEGER): BOOLEAN;
```

This function is similar to `DisplayAlert` except that a standard alert box is used and the text is retrieved from a `'STR#'` resource. If you want to display an alert box, just create a `'STR#'` resource in ResEdit and call this routine with the `'STR#'` resource name and the index in the string list of the string to be used. Whenever possible, this routine should be used instead of `DisplayAlert`. TRUE is returned if the OK button was pressed.

```
PROCEDURE DrawMBarLater (forceItNow: BOOLEAN);
```

The `DrawMBarLater` procedure should be used instead of the Toolbox `DrawMenuBar` procedure. It will collect updates to the menu bar but actually draw the menu bar only when no other events are pending. Using this procedure prevents the menu bar from flashing as menus are added and removed. If the value of `forceItNow` is TRUE, the menu bar is drawn immediately and any pending updates are cleared.

```
FUNCTION  FindOwnerWindow (theRes: Handle): WindowPeek;
```

The `FindOwnerWindow` function checks all of ResEdit's windows to see if an editor is open for the specified resource. If you're writing an editor that uses a resource that may be in use by another editor (for example, two `'DLOG'` resources may share the same `'DITL'`), call `FindOwnerWindow` to determine whether the resource should be released.

```
PROCEDURE FixHand (s: LONGINT; h: Handle);
```

The `FixHand` procedure makes sure that the object to which `h` is a handle is `s` bytes long. If it is longer, `FixHand` shortens it; if it's shorter, `FixHand` expands it and fills the extension with 0.

```
PROCEDURE FlashDialogItem (dp: DialogPtr; item: integer);
```

The `FlashDialogItem` procedure causes a dialog button to blink (inverts the button) for 8 ticks to indicate that the button was selected. This procedure should be called from a dialog's filter procedure.

```
PROCEDURE FrameDialogItem (dp: DialogPtr; item: integer);
```

The `FrameDialogItem` procedure draws a frame around a dialog button to indicate that it is the default button (the button that will be selected when either the Return or the Enter key is pressed). The `dp` parameter is a pointer to the dialog record; `item` is the item number of the button in the corresponding `'DITL'`. This procedure should be called when an update event is received by a dialog's filter procedure.

```
PROCEDURE GetNamedStr(index: INTEGER; name: STR255;
    VAR str: STR255);
```

The `GetNamedStr` procedure returns in `str` the `index`th string in the `'STR#'` resource named `name`. All strings should be stored in either `'STR#'` or `'STR'` resources to maintain the international localizability of ResEdit.

```
FUNCTION GetQuickDrawVars: pQuickDrawVars;
```

This function returns a pointer to the QuickDraw variables that are normally available to Macintosh programmers. Because of the way that pickers and editors are implemented, they do not normally have access to these variables. The following types are used with this function:

```
        pQuickDrawVars = ^QuickDrawVars;
        QuickDrawVArs = RECORD
            randSeed:       LONGINT;
            screenBits:     BitMap;
            arrow:          Cursor;
            dkGray:         Pattern;
            ltGray:         Pattern;
            gray:           Pattern;
            black:          Pattern;
            white:          Pattern;
            thePort:        GrafPtr;
        END; { QuickDrawVars }
```

```
FUNCTION GetScreenRect (roomForIcons: BOOLEAN;
    wind: windowPtr): Rect;
```

The `GetScreenRect` function returns the rectangle of the screen containing most of the specified window. If the value of `roomForIcons` is TRUE, the window is on the main screen, and the screen is large, there is room for the Finder icons at the right edge. If the window is on the main screen, the rectangle returned will not include the menu bar.

```
PROCEDURE GetStr (index, resID: INTEGER; VAR str: STR255);
```

The `GetStr` procedure returns, in `str`, string number `index` from ResEdit's `'STR#'` resource with ID of `resID`. All strings should be stored in either `'STR#'` or `'STR'` resources to maintain the international localizability of ResEdit.

```
FUNCTION HandleCheck (h: Handle; msgID: INTEGER): BOOLEAN;
```

The `HandleCheck` function checks to see if the handle `h` is NIL or empty. If it is either, `HandleCheck` returns FALSE and displays an error alert, using string `msgID` from ResEdit's `'STR#'` resource ID 129. If the handle ID is OK, `HandleCheck` returns TRUE.

```
PROCEDURE MetaKeys (VAR cmd, shift, opt: BOOLEAN);
```

The `MetaKeys` procedure returns the values of the modifier keys from the last event. Some menu commands that have shortcut key combinations simulate the shortcut modifier keys when the menu command is selected. For example, when the user chooses Open Using Template from the Resource menu, `MetaKeys` indicates that the Command and Option modifier keys were pressed. Because of these transformations, `MetaKeys` should always be used to get the modifier values.

```
FUNCTION  PrintSetup: Handle;
```

Use `PrintSetup` if you are doing your own printing instead of using `PrintWindow`. Return type is actually `THPrint`. The following code can be used to set up your own printing loop:

```
myPrintHandle := PrintSetup;
IF myPrintHandle <> NIL THEN
    BEGIN
    PrOpen;
    IF PrError = noErr THEN
      BEGIN
      IF PrJobDialog( myPrintHandle ) THEN
            BEGIN
            printingPort := PrOpenDoc(myPrintHandle, NIL, NIL );
            IF PrError = noErr THEN
                BEGIN
{do the usual printing loop here (see TechNote #161)   }
{Warning: be careful NOT to change the current resfile }
{                    or the printing manager will fail }
                PrCloseDoc( printingPort );
                END;
            END;
      PrClose;
      END;
    END;
```

```
PROCEDURE PrintWindow (toPrint: PicHandle);
```

The `PrintWindow` procedure does just that. If you pass it NIL, it will print an image of the current window. If you pass it a PicHandle, it will print the picture.

```
FUNCTION ResEdID: INTEGER;
```

The `ResEdID` function returns the resource ID of the calling picker or editor. This value should be saved in the `windowKind` field of the editor's window, and also in the `codeResID` field of the `ParentRec` data structure.

```
PROCEDURE SetTheCursor (whichCursor: INTEGER);
```

The `SetTheCursor` procedure changes the cursor to the specified cursor resource. The constant `arrowCursor` defined in the ResEd file should be used to set the cursor to the arrow. The most common use of this routine is to set the cursor to a watch (`watchCursor`) during a time-consuming operation.

```
PROCEDURE ShowInfo (h:Handle; father: ParentHandle);
```

The `ShowInfo` procedure puts up a Get Info window for the resource referenced by `h` that belongs to the father object referenced by `father`. Your editor should call `ShowInfo` when the user chooses Get Info from the File menu.

```
FUNCTION  StandardFilter(theDialog: DialogPtr;
     VAR theEvent: EventRecord; VAR itemHit: INTEGER): BOOLEAN;
```

The `StandardFilter` function can be used by any dialog to make the appropriate responses when the user presses the Return, Enter, Esc, or Command-period keys. Cut, Copy, and Paste are also supported if there are editable fields in the dialog.

```
PROCEDURE TypeToString (t: ResType; VAR s: Str255);
```

The `TypeToString` procedure returns a string consisting of the four characters that make up the `ResType t`.

```
PROCEDURE UseAppRes;
```

The `UseAppRes` procedure sets the current resource file to be the ResEdit Preferences file. If you need to call a Toolbox procedure that looks for resources starting with the current resource file (`GetNewDialog`, for example), you need to call `UseResFile` with the appropriate resource file before you call the Toolbox procedure. Use this routine to restore ResEdit as the current resource file when you're done.

```
FUNCTION WasAborted: BOOLEAN;
```

The `WasAborted` function returns the state of the aborted flag (set by the `Abort` procedure previously described). This function is useful, for example, if you have just called `PassMenu` with a Close command and you want to know if any of the windows that were closed encountered a problem.

Pop-up menus

```
FUNCTION ColorPalettePopupSelect( whichWindow: WindowPtr;
      itemBox: Rect; VAR whichColor: RGBColor;
      CQDishere: BOOLEAN; useColorPicker: BOOLEAN): BOOLEAN;
```

The `ColorPalettePopupSelect` function handles `mouseDown` events in the color palette pop-up menu. Call this procedure whenever you receive a `mouseDown` event in one of your color patches. The `whichWindow` parameter specifies the window containing the pop-up palette, `itemBox` specifies which `Rect` is to be used to draw the color patch, `whichColor` is the `RGBColor` to be used as default, and `CQDishere` is set to TRUE when Color QuickDraw is available. If the value of `useColorPicker` is TRUE, the color picker dialog is displayed rather than the color pop-up palette. On exit, `whichColor` contains the `RGBColor` selected by the user.

```
PROCEDURE DeinstallColorPalettePopup( whichWindow: WindowPtr;
      CQDishere: Boolean );
```

The `DeinstallColorPalettePopup` procedure removes the palette from the window. See `ColorPalettePopupSelect` for an explanation of the parameters. Call this procedure before closing the window.

```
PROCEDURE DoPopup(whichDialog: DialogPtr;
      promptDialogItem, popupDialogItem: integer;
      VAR menuItem: integer; whichMenu: MenuHandle);
```

The `DoPopup` procedure should be called in response to a `mouseDown` event in a pop-up menu. The `whichDialog` parameter specifies the dialog containing the pop-up menu. The `promptDialogItem` parameter specifies the item in the dialog containing the pop-up menu's prompt and `popupDialogItem` is the pop-up menu itself. The `menuItem` parameter is the current setting and also returns the new setting; `whichMenu` specifies the menu to be displayed.

```
PROCEDURE DrawColorPopup( whichWindow: WindowPtr; itemBox: Rect;
      whichColor: RGBColor; CQDishere: BOOLEAN );
```

The `DrawColorPopup` procedure draws the color patch and a drop shadow indicating that this is actually a pop-up menu. Call this procedure for every pop-up palette whenever you need to update the window contents. The `whichWindow` parameter specifies the window containing the pop-up palette, `itemBox` specifies the `Rect` to be used to draw the color patch, `whichColor` is the `RGBColor` to be drawn, and `CQDishere` is set to TRUE when Color QuickDraw is available.

```
PROCEDURE DrawPopup(whichDialog: DialogPtr; whichDialogItem,
    whichMenuItem: integer; whichMenu: MenuHandle);
```

The `DrawPopup` procedure should be called when you receive an update event for a pop-up menu. The `whichDialog` parameter specifies the dialog containing the pop-up menu, `whichDialogItem` is the item number of the pop-up and `whichMenuItem` is the current setting. The `whichMenu` parameter specifies the menu to be drawn.

```
PROCEDURE InstallColorPalettePopup( whichWindow: WindowPtr;
    CQDishere, isActive: BOOLEAN );
```

The `InstallColorPalettePopup` procedure sets up a palette containing the apprpieate set of system colors for the deepest available device, and associates the palette with the window specified by `whichWindow`. Call this procedure immediately after opening your window and whenever you receive an update event. The `CQDishere` parameter should be set to TRUE when Color QuickDraw is available, and `isActive` should be set to TRUE only when the window is the frontmost one.

Internal routines

```
FUNCTION BuildType (t: ResType; l: ListHandle): INTEGER;
```

Given a list that has been initialized with no rows, `BuildType` builds a list of all resources of type `t` from the current resource file. (See the `WindList` routine described in this chapter.) This function requires that the `refCon` field of the list contain the `ParentHandle` of the window owning the list. If `SetResLoad (FALSE)` has not been called, all of the resources will be loaded into memory. The `BuildType` function returns a count of the number of instances that it adds to the list.

A picker that doesn't use `PickerWindSetup` can set up its window with this sequence:
```
myList := WindList(myWindow, myListWidth, myCellSize, ResEdid);
myList^^.refCon := LongInt(myParentHandle);
LDoDraw(FALSE, myList);                {draw it later}
NInsts := BuildType(myType, myList);
LSetSelect(TRUE, Cell(0), myList);     {automatically select first cell}
LDoDraw(TRUE, myList);                 {ok to draw it next time}
```

```
FUNCTION CompressedResource(theResource: Handle): BOOLEAN;
```

The `CompressedResource` function returns TRUE if the specified resource is compressed using the system software release 7.0 compression technique.

```
PROCEDURE DoKeyScan (var evt: EventRecord; offset: integer;
    lh: ListHandle);
```

The `DoKeyScan` procedure is called for you by `PickEvent` and shouldn't be used.

```
FUNCTION DupPick (h: Handle; c: cell; pick: PickHandle):
    Handle;
```

The `DupPick` function is called from `PickMenu` and should normally not need to be called from any other procedures.

```
PROCEDURE GetErrorText (error: INTEGER; VAR errorText:
    STR255);
```

The `GetErrorText` procedure returns an error string for the given error. If no specific error text is found, the text for an I/O error is returned.

```
FUNCTION  GetResEditScrapFile: INTEGER;
```

The `GetResEditScrapFile` function returns the resource file number of the ResEdit scrap file. You can use this procedure if you want to do your own scrap manipulation.

```
FUNCTION GetType (templatesOnly: BOOLEAN; VAR s: STR255):
    BOOLEAN;
```

The `GetType` function displays a dialog box containing a list of the types of resources that can be edited. The list contains all types for which there are templates. If the value of `templatesOnly` is FALSE, the list also contains all the types for which there are editors. The selected type is returned in `s`. TRUE is returned if a type was selected; FALSE is returned otherwise.

```
FUNCTION  MapResourceType (editor: BOOLEAN; theRes: Handle;
    origResType: ResType): ResType;
```

This function checks the `'RMAP'` resources in ResEdit and the ResEdit Preferences file to see if the specified resource type should be treated as if it were of a different type.

```
FUNCTION  PlaySyncSound(which: INTEGER; sndHandle: Handle):
    BOOLEAN;
```

This function is used by the `'snd'` picker to play sounds.

```
FUNCTION ResEditRes: INTEGER;
```

The `ResEditRes` procedure returns the resource file ID of ResEdit. This routine is rarely needed. You can use this routine if you don't want to release a resource that you have been editing, if the resource came from ResEdit.

```
PROCEDURE ResourceIDHasChanged (theObj: ParentHandle;
      theType: ResType; theOldId, theNewId: INTEGER);
```

Call this procedure if you have changed the ID of a resource. If you change a resource ID and don't call this routine, revert won't work properly. The `theObj` parameter is a handle to the parent record of the editor that is editing the changed resource; `theType` is the resource type; `theOldId` and `theNewId` are the ID numbers involved in the change.

```
FUNCTION  RestoreRemovedResources (pick: PickHandle): BOOLEAN;
```

This function reverts all resources of the type handled by the picker (`pick^^.rType`). The `pick` parameter is a handle to the parent record of the picker. This function returns TRUE if the list needs to be rebuilt.

```
PROCEDURE ScrapCopy (theType: ResType; VAR h: Handle );
```

The `ScrapCopy` procedure copies the handle h into the ResEdit scrap. A different handle will be returned. If h isn't a resource, it is added to the scrap with type `theType`.

```
PROCEDURE ScrapEmpty;
```

The `ScrapEmpty` procedure empties the ResEdit and desktop scraps.

```
PROCEDURE SendRebuildToPicker (theType: ResType;
      parent: ParentHandle);
```

This procedure is similar to `SendRebuildToPickerAndFile` except that it doesn't send the rebuild on to the file (what a surprise!).

```
PROCEDURE SendRebuildToPickerAndFile (theType: ResType;
    parent: ParentHandle);
```

This procedure sends a rebuild (sets the rebuild flag in the window's `parentRecord`) to all open picker windows of the specified type. A rebuild is also sent to the file picker in case a new resource type is being added. This routine is useful if an editor creates a resource of another type. The `theType` parameter is the type of resource involved; `parent` is a handle to the parent record of the object that has changed. Editors typically pass their own parent record in this parameter (not the parent record of the picker that launched the editor). This routine should be called to make sure that the resource picker and the file picker are updated to reflect the addition of the new resource. For example, this routine is called from the `'ALRT'`, `'DLOG'`, and `'DITL'` editors.

```
FUNCTION SysResFile: INTEGER;
```

This function returns the resource file ID of the System file. It is often necessary to take special precautions when accessing the System file. This function allows you to take these precautions without hard-coding a value for the system resource file ID, which may change in the future.

```
FUNCTION WindList (w: WindowPtr; nAcross: INTEGER;
    cSize: Point; drawProc:INTEGER): ListHandle;
```

The `WindList` function creates a new empty list and returns a handle to that list.; it should be used by pickers to allocate their lists. This function calls the `LNew` procedure to allocate a list. The `w` parameter specifies the window in which the list will be created, and `nAcross` specifies the number of cells across that the list should contain. The list is allocated with 0 rows. The `cSize` parameter in this function is passed to `LNew` as its `cSize` parameter, and `drawProc` is passed to `LNew` as its `Proc` parameter. For more information on lists and a description of the `LNew` parameters, see the chapter on the List Manager in *Inside Macintosh*, Volume IV.

```
PROCEDURE WindOrigin (w: WindowPtr; dad:ParentHandle);
```

The `WindOrigin` procedure moves the window pointed to by `w` to the correct location on the screen. If `w` is a color window, the window is positioned on the deepest available display device. This routine guarantees that, if possible, the entire window will be visible. This procedure requires that the "windowkind" field of `w` be set to a ResEdit value (for example by a call to `ResEdID`), and that the window size be set. If you are using the `PickerWindSetup` or `EditorWindSetup` procedure, you don't need to call this procedure.

```
PROCEDURE WritePreferences (prefType: ResType;
     prefId: INTEGER; prefName: STR255; prefHandle: Handle);
```

You can use `WritePreferences` to add your own preference resource to the ResEdit Preferences file. The `PrefType` parameter is the resource type that you have chosen for your preference resource. The `prefId` and `prefName` parameters are the ID and name for the resource. The `prefHandle` parameter is a handle to the preference data itself. To read your preferences you can use this code:

```
myPrefs:= Get1NamedResource(prefType, prefName);
```

To conform to ResEdit's standard way of storing preferences, use a type of `'PREF'` and an ID number that's ten times the ID number of your editor.

Appendix A The 'KCHR' Resource

This appendix contains more information about the 'KCHR' resource, its structure, and its function. The 'KCHR' resource controls mapping from the keyboard to the resulting characters. This mapping process involves several areas of the Macintosh architecture.

Basic theory of keyboard operation

In order to appreciate fully the workings of the 'KCHR' editor, you really should be aware of the process that it controls. Here is a summary.

Generating the virtual keycode

Whenever a key on any type of keyboard is pressed, the operating system polls the key information from the device. It then translates each raw keycode generated by the keyboard into a virtual keycode and a combination of modifier keys by means of the 'KMAP' resource. The resulting virtual keycode is information about the key being pressed that is independent of the keyboard type.

Exceptions to the rule

Some countries have different layouts for different keyboards, mostly for historical reasons. To deal with those exceptions, the 'itlk' resource contains a table of translation rules from a virtual keycode generated by the actually connected keyboard to a virtual keycode on the ISO ADB keyboard or to whatever keyboard is supported by the 'KCHR' resource for that country.

Generating the character code

When the operating system has generated a virtual keycode, the `KeyTrans()` procedure then translates the virtual keycode and the concurrently pressed modifier keys into a Macintosh character set number based on the tables in the 'KCHR' resource. That character number and the virtual keycode information are then stored in the event queue and can be accessed by calling `GetNextEvent()`.

Dead keys

When you press a dead key, the first thing you'll notice is that nothing happens immediately (that is, no event is fed into the queue). When you then press another key, the Event Manager uses the character number generated by this new key and the previously pressed dead key to determine which character number should be put in the event queue. This process is used, for example, to generate the German characters with umlauts Ä, Ö, Ü, ä, ö, and ü. You have to press the dead key for a diaeresis (which is Option-u in the U.S. 'KCHR') and then press one of the keys that generate the characters A, O, U, a, o, or u. (You can also generate ï, and ë, which do not exist in German, but, depending on the font, possibly not their uppercase equivalents.) If you press a key that generates none of the defined character numbers for this dead key, the Event Manager generates the nomatch character (which is, in the case discussed here, the umlaut alone).

The Dead Array contains a list of dead keys. For each dead key it defines the virtual keycode and the table that is used to trigger the dead-key mechanism. It then lists pairs of completion characters and substitution characters and, finally, the nomatch characters. The whole dead-key mechanism can be described as follows:

1. Press a dead key on the keyboard.
2. Press any key that generates a character number that corresponds to a valid completion character.

You get the corresponding substitution character in the event queue. (If you didn't press a valid completion character in step 2, you get the nomatch character.)

The structure of a `KCHR` resource

Here is the definition of a `'KCHR'` for the resource compiler Rez. (This information can also be found in the file SysTypes.r in the folder {RIncludes} in MPW.)

```
type 'KCHR' {
   integer;                              /* Version            */
   wide array [$100] {                   /* Indexes            */
      byte;
   };
   integer = $$CountOf(TableArray);
   array TableArray {
      wide array [$80] {                 /* ASCII characters   */
         char;
      };
   };
   integer = $$CountOf(DeadArray);
   array DeadArray {
      byte;                              /* Table number       */
      byte;                              /* Virtual keycode    */
      integer = $$CountOf(CompletorArray);
      wide array CompletorArray {
         char;                           /* Completing char    */
         char;                           /* Substituting char  */
      };
      char;                              /* No match char1     */
      char;                              /* No match char2     */
   };
};
```

Each table in the Table Array describes the virtual keycode-to-character number translation for one complete layer of the keyboard (that is, for all 128 possible keys). The Index Array defines the mapping of modifier key combinations to tables. The high byte of the modifier flag (described in *Inside Macintosh*, Volume V, Chapter 10) is used as an index to determine the number of the table to be used for translation. The information in *Inside Macintosh* is, however, not complete, because the alternate modifier keys (the Shift, Option, and Control keys on the right side of the ADB extended keyboard) are not mentioned. Those keys are normally coupled with the corresponding keys on the left side. It is possible to uncouple them by sending a command to the keyboard. (See "Reassigning Right Key Code" in *Inside Macintosh*, Volume V, Chapter 10.) The correct bit layout of the high byte is shown in Figure A-1.

■ **Figure A-1** Modifier flag high byte

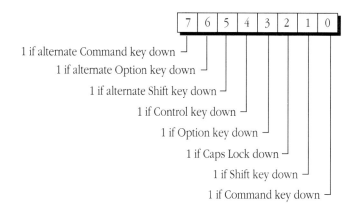

Suppose you hold down the Option key. This keypress will result in a value of 8 (bit 3 is set) in the high byte of the modifier flag. Thus the Toolbox Event Manager takes the value stored in `IndexArray[8]`, which is 3 in the current U.S. 'KCHR', and therefore uses Table 3 to translate the keycodes to character numbers.

Appendix B The `BNDL` Resource

The `BNDL` resource bundles together icons (resource types `ICN#`, `ics#`, `icl4`, `icl8`, `ics4`, `ics8`), file type references (resource type `FREF`), and the "signature" resource (whose resource type is identical to the creator field of the application file) for the Finder. This enables the Finder to display distinct icons for an application and its documents, and also enables it to launch the appropriate application when the user double-clicks a document.

The structure of a 'BNDL' resource

The 'BNDL' resource contains a reference to the signature resource type and ID (for historical reasons the ID must be 0) as well as a list of resource types (almost always only 'FREF' and 'ICN#', although other things are theoretically possible) and localID to resourceID mapping tables. The term *local ID* is used, because this ID is used within the 'BNDL' resource itself to tie together the file reference and its icons. When the Finder copies the 'BNDL' resource and all its bundled resources to the Desktop file (or the desktop database in System 7.0), it actually has to change the resource ID numbers to avoid ID conflicts within the Desktop file. The local ID numbers remain unchanged.

The signature resource can contain anything you want, although, for historical reasons, it typically contains some version and copyright information. The resource ID of the signature resource needs to be 0. If you use the 'BNDL' editor in ResEdit 2.1, this resource is transparently created and maintained for you.

For every file type that should be displayed with a distinct icon in the Finder, there needs to be two entries in the 'BNDL' resource, which in turn refer to one 'FREF' resource, and one 'ICN#' resource (or an entire Finder icon family for system software version 7.0). The 'FREF' resource contains the four-character file type and a reference to a local ID for an icon to be used for this file type. Even if you plan to include an entire icon family, you only need to list the 'ICN#' resource in the 'BNDL' resource. The System 7.0 Finder automatically recognizes and loads all the other parts of the Finder icon family. The relationship of local ID numbers and resource ID numbers is shown in Figure B-1.

■ **Figure B-1** Six resources and their relationships

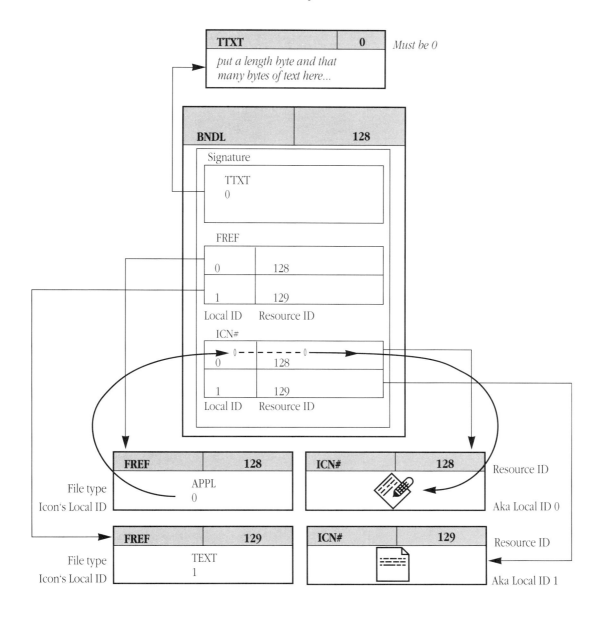

For the Finder to recognize a `BNDL` resource these conditions must be met:

- The bundle must be complete; that is, all the resources listed here must exist and their relationships must be defined. If you use the `BNDL` resource editor built into ResEdit 2.1, you can be sure that this condition is met.
- The file's creator must be identical to the signature specified in the `BNDL` resource and the file's file type must be one listed in the `BNDL` (that is, it must have its own `FREF` and corresponding `ICN#`). Typically the file type will be `APPL` for application, although any file can contain `BNDL` resources. Specific examples other than `APPL` are `INIT` and `CDEV`. Use the Get File/Folder Info command in the File menu to change the file's file type or creator.
- The file's Bundle bit must be set and the Inited bit must be cleared. The Finder always sets the Inited bit whenever it finds a new file and reads in some information about it. By clearing this bit you tell the Finder to reread that information. Use the Get File/Folder Info command in the File menu to change the Bundle and Inited bits.
- There must not already be a `BNDL` resource with the same signature in the Desktop file (or desktop database in System 7.0). If you want to change an existing bundle (to modify the icons, for example), you will need to recreate the Desktop file by rebooting while holding down the Option and Command keys. Note that by doing so, you will lose all comments you may have entered in the Get Info windows in the Finder in system software before version 7.0. Alternatively, you can remove the offending `BNDL` from the Desktop file with ResEdit.

Definitions of the 'BNDL' and 'FREF' resources

Here are the definitions of the 'BNDL' and 'FREF' resources from the MPW Types.R file:

```
/*-------------------------BNDL • Bundle-------------------------*/
type 'BNDL' {
          literal longint;               /* Signature    */
          integer;                       /* Version ID   */
          integer = $$CountOf(TypeArray) - 1;
          array TypeArray {
                    literal longint;     /* Type         */
                    integer = $$CountOf(IDArray) - 1;
                    wide array IDArray {
                         integer;        /* Local ID     */
                         integer;        /* Actual ID    */
                    };
          };
};
/*-------------------FREF • File Reference----------------------*/
type 'FREF' {
          literal longint;               /* File Type    */
          integer;                       /* Icon ID      */
          pstring;                       /* Filename     */
};
```

Appendix C Resource Types Defined for Rez and ResEdit

This appendix contains a list of some resource types in use at Apple Computer, Inc., current as of mid-1990. An attempt has been made to give pertinent information about what each type is, how it is handled by the resource compiler, Rez, and how it is handled by ResEdit. This list is neither formal nor exhaustive.

In some entries, a digit appears to the right of a resource type name. This indicates the particular resource of that type with that ID number.

■ **Table C-1** Resource types defined for Rez and ResEdit

Type	Definition	Rez	ResEdit
`'actb'`	Alert color look-up table	Types.r	Template
`'acur'`	Animated cursor resource	Types.r	Template
`'ADBS'`	ADB driver loaded before `'INIT'` 31	-----	-----
`'ALRT'`	Alert template	Types.r	Template, Editor
`'APPL'`	Application list (Desktop)	-----	Template
`'atpl'`	AppleTalk resource	-----	-----
`'bmap'`	Bitmap	-----	-----
`'BNDL'`	Bundle	Types.r	Template, Editor
`'CACH'`	RAM cache control code	-----	-----
`'cctb'`	Control color look-up table	Types.r	Template
`'CDEF'`	Code for drawing controls	-----	-----
`'cicn'`	Color icon	Types.r	Editor
`'clut'`	Generic color look-up table	Types.r	Template
`'CMDO'`	For MPW commando interface	Cmdo.r	-----
`'cmnu'`	MacApp temporary menu resource	MacAppTypes.r	Editor
`'CNTL'`	Control template	Types.r	Template
`'CODE' 0`	Jump table	-----	-----
`'CODE'`	Application code	-----	-----
`'crsr'`	Color cursor	Types.r	-----
`'ctab'`	Cache tab (list of possible cache sizes)	-----	-----
`'CTY#'`	City list from MAP CDEV	-----	Template
`'CURS'`	Cursor	Types.r	Editor
`'dctb'`	Dialog color look-up table	Types.r	Template
`'DICL'`	(for MacWorkstation)	-----	-----
`'DITL'`	Dialog item list	Types.r	Template, Editor
`'DLOG'`	Dialog template	Types.r	Template, Editor
`'DRVR'`	Driver	SysTypes.r	Template
`'DSAT'`	Startup alerts and code to display them	-----	-----
`'errs'`	MacApp error string	MacAppTypes.r	-----
`'FBTN'`	MiniFinder button	-----	Template
`'fctb'`	Font color look-up table	Types.r	Template
`'FCMT'`	GetInfo comments from Desktop file	-----	Template
`'FDIR'`	MiniFinder button directory ID	-----	Template
`'finf'`	Font information	SysTypes.r	Template
`'FKEY'`	Function Key Code	-----	-----

(Continued)

■ **Table C-1** Resource types defined for Rez and ResEdit (continued)

Type	Definition	Rez	ResEdit
`'fld#'`	List of folder names	SysTypes.r	Template
`'FMTR'`	Format record	-----	-----
`'FOBJ'`	Information about folders	-----	-----
`'FOND'`	Font family description	SysTypes.r	Template
`'FONT'`	Font description	SysTypes.r	Template, Editor
`'FREF'`	File reference	Types.r	Template
`'FRSV'`	ROM font resources	-----	Template
`'FWID'`	Font width table	SysTypes.r	Template
`'gama'`	Gamma table (color correction for screen)	-----	-----
`'GNRL'`	NBP timeout and retry info for AppleTalk	-----	-----
`'ICON'`	Icon	Types.r	Editor
`'ICN#'`	Icon list	Types.r	Editor
`'ictb'`	Color dialog item list	-----	-----
`'INIT'`	Code that is run at system startup time	-----	-----
`'insc'`	Installer script	SysTypes.r	Template
`'INTL'` 0	International formatting information (= `'itl0'`; no longer used)	SysTypes.r	Editor
`'itl0'`	International formatting information	SysTypes.r	Editor
`'INTL'` 1	International date/time information (= `'itl1'`; no longer used)	SysTypes.r	Editor
`'itl1'`	International date/time information	SysTypes.r	Editor
`'itl2'`	International string comparison package hooks	SysTypes.r	-----
`'itl4'`	International tokenize	SysTypes.r	-----
`'itlb'`	International script bundle	SysTypes.r	-----
`'itlc'`	International configuration	SysTypes.r	-----
`'itlk'`	International exception dictionary for kchar	SysTypes.r	Template
`'KCAP'`	Physical layout of keyboard	SysTypes.r	Template
`'KCHR'`	ASCII mapping (software)	SysTypes.r	Editor
`'KEYC'`	old keyboard layout (used by old `'INIT'` 0 and 1)	-----	-----
`'KMAP'`	Keyboard mapping (hardware)	SysTypes.r	Template
`'kscn'`	Keyboard/script icon	Types.r	-----
`'KSWP'`	Keyboard swapping	SysTypes.r	Template
`'LAYO'`	Finder layout resource	-----	Template
`'LDEF'`	Code for drawing lists	-----	-----
`'mach'`	cdev filtering	SysTypes.r	-----
`'MACS'`	Version # in system file	-----	Template

(Continued)

■ **Table C-1** Resource types defined for Rez and ResEdit (continued)

Type	Definition	Rez	ResEdit
`'MBAR'`	Menu bar	Types.r	Template
`'MBDF'`	Menu bar definition procedure (code)	-----	-----
`'mcky'`	Mouse tracking	SysTypes.r	Template
`'mctb'`	Menu color look-up table	Types.r	Editor
`'mcod'`	MacroMaker information	-----	-----
`'mdct'`	MacroMaker information	-----	-----
`'MDEF'`	Code for drawing menus	-----	-----
`'mem!'`	MacApp memory utilization	MacAppTypes.r	-----
`'MENU'`	Menu	Types.r	Template, Editor
`'minf'`	Macro info (MacroMaker)	-----	Template
`'mitq'`	Default queue sizes for `MakeITable`	SysTypes.r	-----
`'mntb'`	MacApp menu table (relate command # to menu)	-----	-----
`'mppc'`	MPP configuration resource	SysTypes.r	-----
`'NBPC'`	NBP configuration (AppleTalk)	-----	-----
`'ncts'`	List of constants	-----	-----
`'NFNT'`	Font description	SysTypes.r	-----
`'nrct'`	Rectangle position list	SysTypes.r	Template
`'PACK'`	Packages of code used as ROM extensions	-----	-----
`'PAPA'`	Printer access protocol address (AppleTalk)	-----	Template
`'PAT'`	QuickDraw pattern	Types.r	Editor
`'PAT#'`	QuickDraw pattern List	Types.r	Editor
`'PDEF'`	Code to drive printers	-----	-----
`'PICT'`	QuickDraw picture	Types.r	Template
`'pltt'`	Color palette	Types.r	Template
`'POST'`	PostScript (in Laser Prep file)	-----	Template
`'ppat'`	Pixel pattern	Types.r	Template
`'ppt#'`	Array of `'ppat's`	-----	-----
`'PREC'`	Printer driver's private data storage	-----	-----
`'PRC0'`	Default page setup info for printer (`'PREC'` 0)	-----	Template
`'PRC3'`	Print record (`'PREC'` 3)	-----	Template
`'PSAP'`	Just a string	-----	Template
`'PTCH'`	ROM patch	-----	-----
`'qrsc'`	System 7.0 query resource	-----	Template
`'res!'`	Resident MacApp segments	MacAppTypes.r	-----
`'ROv#'`	ROM resource override	SysTypes.r	Template
`'scrn'`	Screen configuration	SysTypes.r	Template
`'seg!'`	MacApp memory management	MacAppTypes.r	-----

(Continued)

■ **Table C-1** Resource types defined for Rez and ResEdit (continued)

Type	Definition	Rez	ResEdit
`'SERD'`	RAM serial driver	-----	-----
`'SICN'`	Small icon	Types.r	Editor
`'SIGN'`	?	-----	Template
`'SIZE'`	MultiFinder size information	Types.r	Template
`'snd '`	Sound	SysTypes.r	----- (player)
`'STR '`	Pascal-style string	Types.r	Template
`'STR#'`	Pascal-style string list	Types.r	Template
`'styl'`	Style information for TextEdit	-----	Editor
`'TEXT'`	Unlabeled string	-----	Template, Editor
`'tlst'`	Title list	-----	-----
`'TMPL'`	ResEdit template	-----	Template
`'vers'`	Version	SysTypes.r	Template
`'view'`	MacApp view resource	ViewTypes.r	(ViewEdit, not ResEdit)
`'wctb'`	Window color look-up table	Types.r	Template
`'WDEF'`	Code for drawing windows	-----	-----
`'WIND'`	Window template	Types.r	Template, Editor
`'wstr'`	Query string used by `'qrsc'` resource	-----	Template

Appendix D The Macintosh Character Set

This appendix contains a chart (Figure D-1) that displays the regular character set for Macintosh fonts. The first 128 characters correspond to the standard ASCII character set. Please remember that not all fonts for the Macintosh have these standard characters in them. Specific examples are Symbol and ITC Zapf Dingbats: there are also many pictorial fonts available as bitmaps for dot-matrix printing.

■ **Figure D-1** Macintosh character set

	0	1	2	3	4	5	6	7	8	9	A	B	C	D	E	F
0	nul	dle	sp	0	@	P	`	p	Ä	ê	†		¿	–	‡	
1	soh		!	1	A	Q	a	q	Å	ë	°	±	¡	—	·	Ò
2	stx		"	2	B	R	b	r	Ç	ì	¢	≤	¬	"	,	Ú
3	etx		#	3	C	S	c	s	É	î	£	≥	√	"	„	Û
4	eot		$	4	D	T	d	t	Ñ	ï	§	¥	ƒ	'	‰	Ù
5	enq	nak	%	5	E	U	e	u	Ö	ï	•	μ	≈	'	Â	ı
6	ack	syn	&	6	F	V	f	v	Ü	ñ	¶	∂	Δ	÷	Ê	ˆ
7	bel	etb	'	7	G	W	g	w	á	ó	ß	Σ	«	◊	Á	˜
8	bs	can	(	8	H	X	h	x	à	ò	®	Π	»	ÿ	Ë	¯
9	ht	em	)	9	I	Y	i	y	â	ô	©	π	…	Ÿ	È	˘
A	lf	sub	*	:	J	Z	j	z	ä	ö	™	∫	nbsp	/	Í	˙
B	vt	esc	+	;	K	[	k	{	ã	õ	´	ª	À	¤	Î	˚
C	ff	fs	,	<	L	\	l	|	å	ú	¨	º	Ã	‹	Ï	¸
D	cr	gs	-	=	M	]	m	}	ç	ù	≠	Ω	Õ	›	Ì	˝
E	so	rs	.	>	N	^	n	~	é	û	Æ	æ	Œ	fi	Ó	˛
F	si	us	/	?	O	_	o	del	è	ü	Ø	ø	œ	fl	Ô	ˇ

sp	Space
del	Delete —
nbsp	nonbreaking space (Option-Space on U.S. keyboard)

The key labeled Delete on the U.S. keyboard actually generates backspace (08) character.

▨ The shaded characters cannot normally be generated from the Macintosh keyboard or keypad.

Index

1)***** 96

A

@ABCD 112
`AbleMenu` procedure 133
`Abort` procedure 130
`'actb'` resource type 53
Align To Grid 62
`AlreadyOpen` function 121
ALRT menu 56, 58
`'ALRT'` resource editor 53–59
`'ALRT'` resource type 53, 60, 97
Application Memory Size 96
ascent 49
ASCII character set 50
Auto Position 56

B

Background menu 70
Balloon Help 62
bit editor 4, 28
bit editors 97
Blend 69
`'BNDL'` resource editor 64–67, 152
`'BNDL'` resource type 64, 150
`BubbleUp` procedure 131
`BuildType` function 138
Bundle bit 16, 66, 152

C

`CallDoEvent` procedure 130
`CallInfoUpdate` procedure 130
`'CDEV'` resource type 152
`CenterDialog` procedure 131
character set
    ASCII 50
    Macintosh 2, 50
character-editing panel 49
character-selection panel 50

characters
    Option-space 2
    unprintable 2
`CheckError` function 131
`ChooseIcon` function 132
cicn menu 36
`'cicn'` resource editor 35-36
`'cicn'` resource type 3, 35
Clear 22
Close 13
`CloseNoSave` function 128
clut menu 69
`'clut'` resource editor 68–70
`'clut'` resource type 3, 31, 68
`'cmnu'` resource editor 79
`'cmnu'` resource type 79
CMY Model 69
`'CNTL'` resource type 60
`'CODE'` resource type 2, 19, 108
color-dropper tool 29
Color menu 31
color table record 48
color-dropper tool 29
`ColorAvailable` function 132
`ColorPalettePopupSelect`
    function 137
commands, menu. *See* individual
    command name
Complement 69
`CompressedResource` function
    138
`ConcatStr` procedure 132
Convert To Dead Key 78
Copy 22
corrupted resource 9
crsr menu 34
`'crsr'` resource type 3
CURS menu 34
`'CURS'` resource editor 33
`'CURS'` resource type 3, 33
Cut 22

D

damaged resource 9
data fork 2, 12
`'dctb'` resource type 53
default System font 48
`DefaultListCellSize` function
    126
`DeinstallColorPalettePopup`
    procedure 137
DeRez 5
descent 49
Desktop file 11
    rebuilding 66
dialog box 4
    User Items in 60
dialog item list 59
Dialog Manager 60
`DisplayAlert` function 132
`DisplaySTRAlert` function 133
DITL menu 61
`'DITL'` resource editor 25, 59–64, 97,
    108
`'DITL'` resource type 3, 53, 59, 63,
    96, 97
    associated with `'ALRT'` or
        `'DLOG'` 55
DLOG menu 56, 59
`'DLOG'` resource editor 53–59
`'DLOG'` resource type 3, 53, 60, 96, 97
`DoEvent` procedure 113, 118
`DoInfoUpdate` procedure 116
`DoKeyScan` procedure 139
`DoMenu` procedure 111, 116
`DoPickBirth` function 126
`DoPopup` procedure 137
`DrawColorPopup` procedure 137
`DrawLDEF` procedure 126
`DrawMBarLater` procedure 133
`DrawPopup` procedure 138
`DrawResource` procedure 126

'DRVR' resource type 25
Duplicate 22
Duplicate Table 78
DupPick function 139

E

Edit Dead Key... 78
Edit menu 17–18
EditBirth procedure 111, 115, 118, 129
editors
 bit 28, 97
 hexadecimal 3
 template 3
 upgrading 112–115
 'ALRT' 53–59
 'BNDL' 64–67, 152
 'cicn' 35–36
 'clut' 68–70
 'cmnu' 79
 'CURS' 33
 'DITL' 25, 59–64, 97, 108
 'DLOG' 53–59
 'FONT' 47–50
 'ICN#' 39
 'ICON' 39
 'INTL' 70–71
 'itl0' 70–71
 'itl1' 70–71
 'KCHR' 71–79
 'KCHR' dead-key 71
 'MENU' 79
 'PAT ' 44
 'PAT#' 44
 'pltt' 68–70
 'ppat' 45
 'ppt#' 46
 'SICN' 41–42
 'TEXT '/'styl' 84–85
 'vers' 85
 'WIND' 53–59
Finder icon family 36
EditorWindSetup function 121
eraser tool 29
extensibility of ResEdit 5

F

'fctb' resource type 48
File attributes 16

File Busy bit 16
file info box
 settable flags 16
File Locked bit 16
File menu 13–17
File Protected bit 16
file type 65, 152
file window 11
files
 Desktop 11
 ICON.LDEF 109
 ICON.Pick 109
 ResEdit Preferences 31, 43, 94, 97, 111
 Types.R 153
 XXXX.Edit 109
Finder 11, 99
Finder Flags 16
Finder icon family 36
Finder icon family resource editor 36
FindOwnerWindow function 133
FixHand procedure 133
FlashDialogItem procedure 133
FloatingWindowSetup function 122
folder icon 39
'FOND' resource type 47
Font Manager 48
FONT menu 79
'FONT' resource editor 47–50
'FONT' resource editor: ascent of character 49
'FONT' resource editor: descent of character 49
'FONT' resource type 25, 47
Font/DA Mover 48
fork
 data 2
 resource 2
FrameDialogItem procedure 133
'FREF' resource type 64, 150
functions
 AlreadyOpen 121
 BuildType 138
 CheckError 131
 ChooseIcon 132
 CloseNoSave 128
 ColorAvailable 132

functions (continued)
 ColorPalettePopupSelect 137
 CompressedResource 138
 DefaultListCellSize 126
 DisplayAlert 132
 DisplaySTRAlert 133
 DoPickBirth 126
 DupPick 139
 EditorWindSetup 121
 FindOwnerWindow 133
 FloatingWindowSetup 122
 GetQuickDrawVars 134
 GetResEditScrapFile 139
 GetSScreenRect 134
 GetType 139
 HandleCheck 134
 IsThisYours 112
 MapResourceType 139
 NeedToRevert 128
 PickerWindSetup 123
 PickStdHeight 127
 PickStdWidth 127
 PlaySyncSound 139
 PrintSetup 135
 REAddNewRes 124
 REBeautifulUnique1ID 124
 RECount1Resources 124
 RECount1Types 124
 REGet1IndResource 124
 REGet1NamedResource 125
 REGet1Resource 125
 REGet1ResourceSpecial 125
 RENewUniqueRes 125
 ResEdID 135
 ResEditRes 140
 RestoreRemovedResources 140
 RevertThisResource 126
 StandardFilter 136
 SysResFile 141
 WasAborted 136
 WasItLoaded 128
 WindAlloc 123
 WindList 141

G

general editor. *See* hexadecimal editor
Get File/Folder Info 14

Get Info for This File 14
Get Info window 20
`GetErrorText` procedure 139
`GetNamedStr` procedure 134
`GetNewDialog` 111
`GetQuickDrawVars` procedure 134
`GetResEditScrapFile` function 139
`GetStr` function 134
`GetStr` procedure 134
`GetType` function 139
`GetWindowTitle` procedure 122
`GiveEBirth` procedure 129
`GiveSubEBirth` procedure 129
`GiveThisEBirth` procedure 129
graphic resource 4
graphical resource editor 28
graphics tools panel 50
Grid Settings 62
`GrowMyWindow` procedure 127

H

`HandleCheck` procedure 134
hardware requirements xii
hexadecimal editor 4, 52
HLS Model 69
HSB Model 69

I, J

'`icl4`' resource type 3, 36
'`icl8`' resource type 3, 36
'`ICN#`' resource editor 39
'`ICN#`' resource picker 21
'`ICN#`' resource type 3, 36, 39, 65, 98, 150
icon 4
Icon menu 38
'`ICON`' resource editor 39
'`ICON`' resource type 3, 29, 39, 60
Icon Vert. phase 102
ICON.LDEF file 109
ICON.Pick file 109
icons
 folder 39
 monochrome 38
 Trash 39
'`ics#`' resource type 3, 36
'`ics4`' resource type 3, 36
'`ics8`' resource type 3, 36

ID number
 local 150
 resource 150
ID number restriction 25
'`INIT`' resource type 152
Inited bit 66
`InstallColorPalettePopup` procedure 138
'`INTL`' resource editor 70–71
'`INTL`' resource type 70
`IsThisYours` function 112
'`itl0`' resource editor 70–71
'`itl0`' resource type 70
'`itl1`' resource editor 70–71
'`itl1`' resource type 70

K

'`KCHR`' dead-key editor 71
KCHR menu 77, 105
'`KCHR`' resource editor 71–79
'`KCHR`' resource type 71, 105–106, 144–147, 153
'`KCHR`' with Macintosh SE, Macintosh Plus, or Macintosh 512K enhanced 79
'`KMAP`' resource type 144

L

lasso tool 29
'`LAYO`' resource type 4, 88, 99
'`LDEF`' resource type 108
list separator 94
Load Colors 69
local ID number 150

M

MacApp
 permanent menu 79
 temporary menu 79
Macintosh character set 2, 50
Macintosh Programmer's Workshop 5
`MapResourceType` function 139
marquee tool 29
mask 38
'`MBAR`' resource type 99
'`mctb`' resource type 79
'`MDEF`' resource type 83
'`MDPL`' resource type 12, 96

memory requirements xii
'`MENU`' resource editor 79
'`MENU`' resource ID 99
'`MENU`' resource type 79
menus
 ALRT 56, 58
 Background 70
 cicn 36
 clut 69
 Color 31
 crsr 34
 CURS 34
 DITL 61
 DLOG 56, 59
 Edit 17–18
 File 13–17
 FONT 79
 Icon 38
 KCHR 77, 105
 MiniScreen 53
 PAT 42
 ppat 42
 ppt# 42
 PAT# 42
 Resource 18
 SIZE 79
 Sort 70
 Style 81
 Transform 30
 View 23–24
 WIND 56
 Window 22–23
`MetaKeys` procedure 135
MiniScreen menu 53
monochrome icon 38
MPW DeRez command 92
MPW resource compiler and decompiler 5
MultiFinder 11, 99

N

`NeedToRevert` function 128
Never Use Custom '`WDEF`' for Drawing 57, 59
New 13
New Table 78
'`NFNT`' resource type 3, 47
`NoDoubleClickHere` procedure 128

O

Open 13
Open Special 13
Open Using Template 22
Option key 52, 60
Option-space character 2

P

Page Setup 14
paint bucket tool 29
`ParamText` procedure 63
parent record definition 119
`PassEvent` procedure 130
`PassMenu` procedure 130
Paste 22
PAT menu 42
'PAT' resource type 3
'PAT' resource editor 44
'PAT' resource type 42, 44
PAT# menu 42
'PAT#' resource editor 44
'PAT#' resource type 3, 42, 44
pencil tool 29
'PICK' resource type 109, 112, 115
`PickBirth` procedure 115
picker record definition 120
pickers 108
   'ICN#' 21
   'PICT' 97
`PickerWindSetup` function 123
`PickEvent` procedure 116, 127
`PickInfoUp` procedure 127
`PickMenu` procedure 127
`PickStdHeight` function 127
`PickStdWidth` function 127
'PICT' picker 97
'PICT' resource type 12, 29, 60, 89, 96, 97
pictorial resource 4
pictorial resource editor 28
Pictorial resource type 28
Pig mode 98
pixel editor 28
`PlaySyncSound` function 139
pltt menu 69
'pltt' resource editor 68–70
'pltt' resource type 3, 68
PostRez 79

ppat menu 43
'ppat' resource editor 46
'ppat' resource type 3, 43, 46
ppt# menu 42
'ppt#' resource editor 46
'ppt#' resource type 3, 42, 46
'PREF' resource type 142
Preferences 14
   storing 142
Preview at Full Size 56
Print 14
Printer Driver Is MultiFinder
   Compatible bit 16
`PrintSetup` function 135
`PrintWindow` procedure 135
procedures
   `AbleMenu` 131
   `Abort` 130
   `BubbleUp` 131
   `CallDoEvent` 130
   `CallInfoUpdate` 130
   `CenterDialog` 131
   `ConcatStr` 132
   `DeinstallColorPalettePop up` 137
   `DoEvent` 111, 116
   `DoInfoUpdate` 116
   `DoKeyScan` 139
   `DoMenu` 111, 116
   `DoPopup` 137
   `DrawColorPopup` 137
   `DrawLDEF` 126
   `DrawMBarLater` 133
   `DrawPopup` 138
   `DrawResource` 126
   `EditBirth` 111, 115, 118, 129
   `FixHand` 133
   `FlashDialogItem` 133
   `FrameDialogItem` 133
   `GetErrorText` 139
   `GetNamedStr` 134
   `GetStr` 134
   `GetWindowTitle` 122
   `GiveEBirth` 129
   `GiveSubEBirth` 129
   `GiveThisEBirth` 129
   `GrowMyWindow` 127

procedures (continued)
   `InstallColorPalettePopup` 138
   `MetaKeys` 135
   `NoDoubleClickHere` 128
   `ParamText` 63
   `PassEvent` 130
   `PassMenu` 130
   `PickBirth` 115
   `PickEvent` 116, 127
   `PickInfoUp` 127
   `PickMenu` 127
   `PrintWindow` 135
   `REAddResource` 124
   `REGet1IndType` 125
   `RERemoveAnyResource` 125
   `ResourceIDHasChanged` 140
   `ScrapCopy` 140
   `ScrapEmpty` 140
   `SendRebuildToPicker` 140
   `SendRebuildToPickerAndFile` 141
   `SetETitle` 123
   `SetResChanged` 128
   `SetTheCursor` 136
   `ShowInfo` 136
   `TypeToString` 136
   `UseAppRes` 136
   `WindOrigin` 141
   `WindReturn` 123
   `WritePreferences` 142

Q

Quit 14

R

RAM requirements xii
`REAddNewRes` function 124
`REAddResource` procedure 124
`REBeautifulUnique1ID` function 124
rebuilding a Desktop file 66
`RECount1Resources` function 114, 124
`RECount1Types` function 114, 124
`REGet1IndResource` function 114, 124
`REGet1IndType` procedure 114, 125

REGet1NamedResource function 114, 125
REGet1Resource function 114, 125
REGet1ResourceSpecial function 114, 125
Relative Patterns 43
Remove Dead Key 78
Remove Duplicate Tables 78
Remove Unused Tables 78
RENewUniqueRes function 125
Renumber Items 61
RERemoveAnyResource procedure 125
ResEd 5, 110
ResEdID function 135
ResEdit Preferences file 31, 43, 94, 97, 111
ResEditRes function 140
resource 4
resource file checking 9
resource fork 2
resource ID number 25, 150
Resource Map Is Read Only bit 16
Resource menu 18
resource picker 21
resource type name 2
resource types 21
   'actb' 53
   'ALRT' 53, 60, 97
   'BNDL' 64, 150
   'CDEV' 152
   'cicn' 3, 35
   'clut' 3, 31, 68
   'cmnu' 79
   'CNTL' 60
   'CODE' 2, 19, 108
   'crsr' 3
   'CURS' 3, 33
   'dctb' 53
   'DITL' 3, 53, 59, 63, 96, 97
   'DLOG' 3, 53, 60, 96, 97
   'DRVR' 25
   'fctb' 48
   'FOND' 47
   'FONT' 25, 47
   'FREF' 64, 150
   'icl4' 3, 36
   'icl8' 3, 36
   'ICN#' 3, 36, 39, 65, 98, 150
   'ICON' 3, 29, 39, 60

resource types (continued)
   'ics#' 3, 36
   'ics4' 3, 36
   'ics8' 3, 36
   'INIT' 152
   'INTL' 70
   'itl0' 70
   'itl1' 70
   'KCHR' 71, 105-106, 144-147, 153
   'KMAP' 144
   'LAYO' 4, 88, 99
   'LDEF' 108
   'MBAR' 99
   'mctb' 79
   'MDEF' 83
   'MDPL' 12, 96
   'MENU' 79
   'NFNT' 3, 47
   'PAT ' 3
   'PAT' 42, 44
   'PAT#' 3, 42, 44
   'PICK' 109, 112, 115
   'PICT' 12, 29, 60, 89, 96, 97
   'pltt' 3, 68
   'ppat' 3, 42, 45
   'ppt#' 3, 42, 46
   'PREF' 142
   'RMAP' 37, 98
   'RSSC' 108, 110, 118
   'SICN' 3, 41, 82
   'STR#' 63, 91
   'styl 84
   'styl' 3
   'TEXT' 84
   'TMPL' 88, 91
   'vers' 3, 48, 67, 85
   'wctb' 53
   'WIND' 53
ResourceIDHasChanged procedure 140
resources 2
   corrupted 9
   damaged 9
   pictorial 4
   signature 67
RestoreRemovedResources function 140
Revert File 13
RevertThisResource function 126

Rez 5
RGB Model 69
'RMAP' resource type 37, 98
ROM requirements xii
'RSSC' resource type 108, 110, 118

S

sample text panel 51
Save 13
ScrapCopy procedure 140
ScrapEmpty procedure 140
Select Item Number 61
SendRebuildToPicker procedure 140
SendRebuildToPickerAndFile procedure 141
Set 'ALRT' Stage Info... 58
Set 'DLOG' Characteristics... 59
Set 'WIND' Characteristics... 56
SetETitle procedure 123
SetResChanged procedure 128
SetTheCursor procedure 136
Show All Items 62
Show Bottom & Right 56
Show Height & Width 56
Show Item Numbers 62
ShowInfo procedure 136
'SICN' resource editor 41–42
'SICN' resource type 3, 41, 82
signature resource 67
SIZE menu 79
software requirements xii
Sort menu 70
StandardFilter function 136
storing preferences 142
'STR#' resource type 63, 91
straight quotation mark 2
'styl' resource type 3, 84
Style menu 81
Subeditor 108, 129
SysResFile function 141

T

template 4, 5, 22
template editor 3
'TEXT' resource type 84
'TEXT'/'styl' resource editor 84–85
'TMPL' resource type 88, 91

tools
- color-dropper 36
- color-dropper 29
- eraser 29
- lasso 29
- marquee 29
- paintbucket 29
- pencil 29

Transform menu 30
Trash icon 39
Try Pointer 34
type checking 93
Types.R file 153
`TypeToString` procedure 136

U

Uncouple Modifier Keys 77
Undo 22
unprintable character 2
Use Color Picker 56
Use Item's Rectangle 64
`UseAppRes` procedure 139
USES declaration 112

V

Verify Resource File 10, 14
'vers' resource editor 85
'vers' resource type 3, 48, 67, 85
View As... 62, 77
View menu 23–24

W

`WasAborted` function 136
`WasItLoaded` function 128
'wctb' resource type 53
WIND menu 56
'WIND' resource editor 53–59
'WIND' resource type 53
`WindAlloc` function 123
`WindList` function 141
`WindOrigin` procedure 141
Window menu 22–23
windows
- file 11
- Get Info 20

`WindReturn` procedure 123
`WritePreferences` procedure 142

X, Y, Z

XXXX.Edit file 109

THE APPLE PUBLISHING SYSTEM

This Apple manual was written, edited, and composed on a desktop publishing system using Apple Macintosh® computers and Microsoft® Word software. Proof and final pages were created on Apple LaserWriter® printers. Line art was created using Adobe Illustrator™. POSTSCRIPT®, the page-description language for the LaserWriter, was developed by Adobe Systems Incorporated. Screen shots were taken with version 1.3 of FlashIt.

Text type and display type are Apple's corporate font, a condensed version of Garamond. Bullets are ITC Zapf Dingbats®. Some elements, such as program listings, are set in Apple Courier.

Writer: Jon Singer
Developmental Editor: 1.2-Silvio Orsino; 2.0-Steve Hiatt; 2.1-Antonio Padial
Illustrator: Sandee Karr
Production Supervisor: Janet M. Anders

Special thanks to:

Nobu Toge for FlashIt.

Mikel Evins for DreadEdit.

The ResEdit engineering team, particularly Peter, Craig, and Alexander, who helped the author more than he can say.

Doris Wells-Papanek for ResEdit's icons.

The Bazilian family for food and comfort in time of need.

Developer Technical Support at Apple for assistance above and beyond the call of nature, and for Clarus the DogCow, who was modified by Annette Wagner from the dog in the Cairo font. Moof!™